BrightRED Study Guide

Curriculum for Excellence

N5

FRENCH

Orla Herron and Lisa Albarracin

First published in 2013 by:
Bright Red Publishing Ltd
1 Torphichen Street
Edinburgh
EH3 8HX

New edition first published in 2015. Reprinted with corrections 2017.

A CIP record for this book is available from the British Library

ISBN 978-1-906736-82-8

With thanks to:
PDQ Digital Media Solutions Ltd (layout), Alex Hepworth (copy-edit) and Jérôme Lestienne (French language check)

Cover design and series book design by Caleb Rutherford – e i d e t i c

Acknowledgements
Every effort has been made to seek all copyright holders. If any have been overlooked, then Bright Red Publishing will be delighted to make the necessary arrangements.

Permission has been sought from all relevant copyright holders and Bright Red Publishing are grateful for the use of the following:

auremar/Shutterstock.com (p 7); Andresr/Shutterstock.com (p 8); Lucky Business/Shutterstock.com (p 9); Sebastian Gauert/Shutterstock.com (p 10); Valua Vitaly/Shutterstock.com (p 12); Monkey Business Images/Shutterstock.com (p 15); Catherine Murray/Shutterstock.com (p 17); CWA Studios/Shutterstock.com (p 20); Nicholas Piccillo/Shutterstock.com (p 22); Jag_cz/Shutterstock.com (p 22); Dima Fadeev/Shutterstock.com (p 24); jim daly/Stock-Xchnge (p 25); Africa Studio/Shutterstock.com (p 26); Wallenrock/Shutterstock.com (p 30); Aleksandr Bryliaev/Shutterstock.com (p 32); haider/Shutterstock.com (p 32); iQoncept/Shutterstock.com (p 32); ollyy/Shutterstock.com (p 32); conrado/Shutterstock.com (p 32); Miguel A/Shutterstock.com (p 32); Lario Tus/Shutterstock.com (p 33); Countdown Studio (public domain) (p 33); Oleg Zabielin/Shutterstock.com (p 33); Barnaby Chambers/Shutterstock.com (p 33); Jetrel/Shutterstock.com (p 33); ventdusud/Shutterstock.com (p 33); Sergey Nivens/Shutterstock.com (p 33); Lisa F. Young/Shutterstock.com (p 33); Lorelyn Medina/Shutterstock.com (p 33); iQoncept/Shutterstock.com (p 33); Sam72/Shutterstock.com (p 33); saswell/Shutterstock.com (p 33); BonD80/Shutterstock.com (p 34); Helga Esteb/Shutterstock.com (p 36); romrf/Shutterstock.com (p 38); Makhnach_S/Shutterstock.com (p 40); Natalia Klenova/Shutterstock.com (p 41); S.Borisov/Shutterstock.com (p 41); Liudmila Gridina/Shutterstock.com (p 48); Ranglen/Shutterstock.com (p 48); Photographee.eu/Shutterstock.com (p 48); l i g h t p o e t/Shutterstock.com (p 50); wavebreakmedia/Shutterstock.com (p 53); wavebreakmedia/Shutterstock.com (p 55); Syda Productions/Shutterstock.com (p 60); gualtiero boffi/Shutterstock.com (p 60); CandyBox Images/Shutterstock.com (p 62); Andrey_Popov/Shutterstock.com (p 64); auremar/Shutterstock.com (p 70); Marcel Mooij/Shutterstock.com (p 74); Matthew Egginton/Shutterstock.com (p 74); S.Borisov/Shutterstock.com (p 75); Maxim Blinkov/Shutterstock.com (p 75); Sergey Nivens/Shutterstock.com (p 80); CandyBox Images/Shutterstock.com (p 81); Syda Productions/Shutterstock.com (p 87); Kolett/Shutterstock.com (p 88); gpointstudio/Shutterstock.com (p 92).

Printed and bound in the UK.

CONTENTS

BRIGHTRED STUDY GUIDE: NATIONAL 5 FRENCH

SOCIETY

LEARNING

EMPLOYABILITY

CULTURE

COURSE ASSESSMENT

WRITING

LISTENING

APPENDICES

INTRODUCING NATIONAL 5 FRENCH

During this course you will further develop your linguistic knowledge and apply skills for learning, for life and for work purposes.

Learning any language will help you to develop your literacy skills both in the foreign language and English, and improve your cultural knowledge about other countries.

THE NATIONAL 5 FRENCH COURSE

National 5 French encourages you to become a more confident learner; a responsible citizen with an informed and ethical view of other cultures and traditions in Francophone countries; someone who can work independently as well as participate in group discussions and team work.

COURSE ASSESSMENT

The course assessment at National 5 has five components as outlined below.

Component	Mark	Scaled Mark	Duration
Component 1: question paper 1 Reading	30	30	1 Hour and 30 minutes (for paper 1 – Reading and Writing)
Component 2: question paper 1 Writing	20	15	See above
Component 3: question paper 2 Listening	20	30	Approximately 30 minutes
Component 4: assignment – Writing	20	15	No set time limit – centres to use their discretion
Component 5: Performance – Talking	30	30	Approximately 6–8 minutes

COMPONENTS 1, 2 AND 3: READING AND WRITING; LISTENING

In these components, you will be assessed on all four contexts: society, learning, employability and culture. The question papers for Components 1, 2 and 3 are set and marked by SQA and conducted in your school/college/university under exam conditions in either May or June.

QUESTION PAPER 1 – READING AND WRITING (50 MARKS)

This question paper will assess the skills of reading and writing. The question paper will have two sections:

- reading – 30 marks
- writing – 20 marks, scaled mark 15

Section 1 (reading)

You will read three texts and demonstrate your understanding by providing answers in English to the questions asked.

Each text will be based on one of the four contexts (society, learning, employability, culture) and all the texts will be of equal length and difficulty.

ONLINE

The SQA website gives more detail on the grammar and topics that you will need to know about. Follow the link from www.brightredbooks.net/N5French

ONLINE

This book is supported by the BrightRED Digital Zone. Log in at www.brightredbooks.net/N5French to unlock a world of videos, links, tests and much more!

DON'T FORGET

Whilst covering the context and topics in each chapter, you will develop your language skills, increase your vocabulary and be given the opportunity to revise grammatical structures. After each topic you will be asked to use the language learned to write a short essay about the topic. This should help you to consolidate the language learned and you may also wish to use these essays to help prepare your Performance (talking) as part of the external examination.

contd

This section is worth a total of 30 marks, with each text being worth 10 marks. There will be 1–2 supported marks in each text, with one of these total 3–6 supported marks being an overall purpose question.

There will be a variety of question styles and you will be allowed to use a dictionary.

Section 2 (writing)

You will be required to write an email of 120–150 words in French in response to a job advert. There will be four predictable bullet points and two less predictable bullet points. You should have prepared for this thoroughly beforehand and should feel fully equipped to tackle this paper. You will, however, be allowed to use a dictionary.

For help with this section, refer to pages 84–95 of this book.

QUESTION PAPER 2 – LISTENING (20 MARKS, SCALED MARK 30)

You will listen to one monologue in French worth 8 marks and one short conversation in French worth 12 marks. You will demonstrate your understanding by providing short answers in English to the questions asked.

This paper will be based on the context which was not covered in Question paper 1, for example if the reading texts cover society, culture and learning then the listening paper will be on employability.

Find out more about the listening paper on pages 96–101.

Read about Components 4 and 5 on pp 82–83 of this book.

HOW THIS BOOK CAN HELP YOU

BrightRED Study Guide: National 5 French focuses on your work in the year leading up to the examination. It offers you a study 'toolkit' containing: topic-by-topic revision of the National 5 course; progression through contexts and suggested topics; development of language skills; effective techniques for handling exam questions and a range of ways to revise, either on your own or with friends.

Chapter 1: Society	Chapter 2: Learning	Chapter 3: Employability	Chapter 4: Culture	Chapter 5: Writing
Society covers the language needed to discuss relationships with family and friends; healthy lifestyles and illnesses related to a unhealthy lifestyle; media and the impact of reality shows and new technology on our lives; citizenship and the importance of learning foreign languages; the environment and the differences between town and country life and your local area as a tourist centre.	Learning covers the language needed to discuss education and exam preparation; different education systems and responsibilities of learners.	Employability covers the language needed to discuss different jobs, including part-time work; cover letters, CVs and job applications and reviewing achievements and evaluating experiences.	Culture covers the language needed to discuss your best holiday/trip; the importance of travelling; aspects of other countries, including special events and occasions and literature/films.	Writing covers the language you will need to allow you to feel fully prepared for the Writing paper in the exam. This includes personal details (name, age, where you live); school/college education experience until now; skills/interests you have which make you right for the job; related work experience and possible examples of the two unpredictable bullet points.

BEYOND THE EXAM

Not only will this book help you to prepare for and do well in National 5 French, it will also help lay down the skills you will need to do well next year if you decide to continue with Higher French or study a new foreign language at Higher or National 5, take Modern Languages for Work Purposes Units, go into further study or training, or simply continue into the world of work.

 DON'T FORGET

It is now up to you. We hope this book will prove useful and help prepare you fully for both the Unit and Course assessments. Bonne chance!

FAMILY AND FRIENDS – LA FAMILLE ET LES AMIS 1

The Society context can cover a wide range of topics. We will look at each topic in turn within this context and develop your 'toolkit' of language skills, knowledge of vocabulary and grammar. The themes will include:

- relationships with family and friends
- conflicts at home
- healthy lifestyles
- lifestyle-related illnesses
- media
- technology
- life in town compared to life in the countryside
- your home area as a tourist centre
- environment.

LET'S GET STARTED!

Let's start with the subject of family and friends. Can you think of what you would like to be able to say about your relationships with your family and friends?

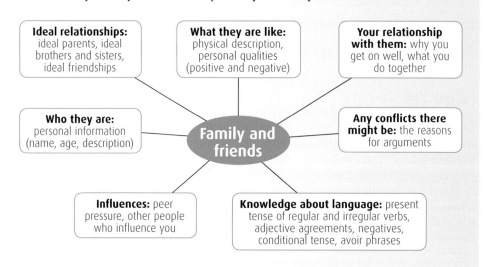

Ideal relationships: ideal parents, ideal brothers and sisters, ideal friendships

What they are like: physical description, personal qualities (positive and negative)

Your relationship with them: why you get on well, what you do together

Who they are: personal information (name, age, description)

Family and friends

Any conflicts there might be: the reasons for arguments

Influences: peer pressure, other people who influence you

Knowledge about language: present tense of regular and irregular verbs, adjective agreements, negatives, conditional tense, avoir phrases

YOUR FAMILY AND FRIENDS, WHO ARE THEY? – TA FAMILLE ET TES AMIS, C'EST QUI?

Quiz

Can you remember the vocabulary in French for the following?

- Members of the family
- What he or she is called
- What age someone is (don't forget to use *avoir* for age!)
- Numbers, days and months
- When someone's birthday is

DON'T FORGET

This is a perfect opportunity to revise vocabulary that you have previously learned.

THE PRESENT TENSE – LE PRÉSENT

When talking about your family relationships, you will mostly use the **present tense**. There are **regular** and **irregular verbs** that you will need to know. Take the following steps to form regular verbs:

1. Write down the subject (the person or thing doing the verb).

2. Write down the **infinitive** without the 'er', 'ir' or 're' ending (this is known as the stem of the **verb**).

3. Add the present tense ending (this must correspond to the subject).

> **EXAMPLE**
>
> *Jouer* – to play (this is known as the infinitive)
>
> Chop off the 'er' to form the stem: *jou*
>
> Write down the subject and the root and add the correct 'er' verb ending: I play
> – *Je jou**e***

ONLINE TEST

Take the test 'Can you remember all the endings for regular 'er', 'ir' and 're' verbs?' at www.brightredbooks.net/N5French

VIDEO LINK

Check out the clip 'Avec la famille' at www.brightredbooks.net/N5French

IRREGULAR VERBS – LES VERBES IRRÉGULIERS

Let's move on to irregular verbs. You need to know these off by heart as they do not follow a pattern. The most important ones that you must learn are:

avoir – to have	vouloir – to want to	partir – to leave
être – to be	pouvoir – to be able to/can	sortir – to go out
aller – to go	devoir – to have to/must	
faire – to do/make	savoir – to know how to	

THINGS TO DO AND THINK ABOUT

Now that you are a 'present tense expert', make up 12 sentences using the present tense. Include the following verbs in your sentences:

a regular 'er' verb	faire
a regular 'ir' verb	vouloir
a regular 're' verb	pouvoir
avoir	devoir
être	partir
aller	sortir

FAMILY AND FRIENDS – LA FAMILLE ET LES AMIS 2

WHAT IS HE/SHE LIKE? – COMMENT EST-IL/ELLE?

You might want to describe what members of your family or your friends look like. Try to think back to when you learned to describe someone's height, hair and eyes.

> **EXAMPLE**
>
> Ma mère est petite, ma sœur a les cheveux noirs.

It is also useful to be able to describe what someone's personality is like. Let's start with the positives.

Learning vocabulary

Firstly, read through the following adjectives and cover up the English meanings. If you know some words already, put a tick or a green mark beside these words. If there are some words that you think you could guess because they look like English words, put a dash or an orange mark beside these words. Be careful, some of them might be **false friends**!

If there are some words that you don't recognise, put a cross or a red mark beside these words and, when doing your revision, spend more time going over and learning these words.

You can listen to these adjectives online to help you with the pronunciation.

Positive adjective	English meaning
aimable	pleasant
amusant(e)	fun
bavard(e)	chatty
compréhensif(-ive)	understanding
disponible	available
doux(-ce)	gentle
drôle	funny
généreux(-euse)	generous
gentil(le)	nice, kind
intelligent(e)	intelligent
ouvert(e)	open
patient(e)	patient
plein(e) de vie	full of life
rigolo(te)	funny
sage	sensible
sensible	sensitive
vif(-ve)	lively

 ACTIVITY NEGATIVES – LES NÉGATIFS

You can use any of these **adjectives** in a negative sentence. All you need to do is put *ne* before the verb (this changes to *n'* if the verb begins with a vowel or a silent 'h') and put the negative word (pas) after the verb.

Here is a reminder of some useful **negatives**. Translate the following sentences and then try to make up five phrases using negative constructions and positive adjectives.

> Ne ... pas – not
> Mon frère aîné n'est pas patient.

contd

Ne ... jamais – never
Ma mère n'est jamais vive.

Ne ... plus – not any more
Mon père n'est plus casse-pieds, il m'écoute.

Ne ... que – only
Ma sœur cadette n'est amusante qu'avec ses amis.

Ne ... personne – no-one
Personne n'est compréhensif chez moi.

Ne ... rien – nothing
Ma sœur aînée n'est pas généreuse, elle ne me donne rien.

NEGATIVE ADJECTIVES – LES ADJECTIFS NÉGATIFS

Once you feel confident with these phrases, move on to the negative adjectives.

Negative adjective	English meaning
antipathique	unpleasant
arrogant(e)	arrogant
autoritaire	bossy
bête	stupid
casse-pieds	annoying
démodé(e)	old-fashioned
égoïste	selfish
embêtant(e)	annoying
ennuyeux(-euse)	boring
fainéant(e)	lazy
gâté(e)	spoilt
grincheux(-euse)	grumpy
impatient(e)	impatient
irritant(e)	irritating
méchant(e)	mean
paresseux(-euse)	lazy
pénible	a nuisance
puéril(e)	childish
sévère	strict

You might like to add some **qualifiers/intensifiers**:

assez – quite	vraiment – really
un peu – a bit	trop – too
très – very	

ONLINE TEST

Take the 'Negative and positive adjectives' test online at www.brightredbooks.net/N5French.

VIDEO LINK

Watch the 'Family and relationships' clip at www.brightredbooks.net/N5French

THINGS TO DO AND THINK ABOUT

Write a paragraph about the members of your family and include names, ages, birthdays and physical descriptions. This could be used as part of your Performance and it is worthwhile revision.

Write a second paragraph about what each member of your family is like. Don't forget to use negatives and qualifiers in your writing.

RELATIONSHIPS – LES RELATIONS

Think about why you get on well with members of your family or friends and why you sometimes argue with them. It would be useful to learn these important phrases to help you describe your relationships.

POSITIVE RELATIONSHIPS – LES RAPPORTS POSITIFS

- J'ai une bonne relation avec ... – I have a good relationship with ...
- J'ai un bon rapport avec ... – I have a good relationship with ...
- Je m'entends bien avec ... – I get on well with ...
- Je me sens proche de ... – I feel close to ...

It is useful to be able to say why you get on well with family members and friends. Here are some phrases to help:

- ... car/parce que/ parce qu'...
- mon père/ma mère/ mon frère/ma sœur est + positive adjective
- il/elle est + adjective

 **ACTIVITY** POSITIVE RELATIONSHIPS – LES RAPPORTS POSITIFS

Read the following French phrases and match them to the English meanings. You can listen to these phrases online to help you with pronunciation.

on s'intéresse aux mêmes choses	we spend a lot of time together
on partage les mêmes intérêts	he/she is very respectful of my private life
on a beaucoup de choses en commun	he/she respects me
il/elle a un bon sens de l'humour	we share the same interests
on passe beaucoup de temps ensemble	he/she supports me when I have a problem
on fait tout ensemble	he/she is always in a good mood

contd

on sort souvent ensemble	he/she helps me when I need it
on partage de bons moments	we can discuss everything
il/elle est toujours de bonne humeur	we do everything together
on rigole	we are interested in the same things
on peut discuter de tout	we have a lot of things in common
il/elle me respecte	we share good times together
on est très proche	we often go out together
il/elle est très respectueux(-euse) de ma vie privée	we have a laugh
il/elle m'aide quand j'en ai besoin	he/she has a good sense of humour
il/elle me soutient quand j'ai un problème	we are very close

DON'T FORGET

You must check adjective agreements, see page 8, for example *mon frère est rigolo/ma soeur est rigolote.*

ACTIVITY: PARENTAL RELATIONSHIPS – LES RELATIONS AVEC SES PARENTS

Read the text below first and look up any words you don't know in the dictionary. Then try to predict what you might hear and think of any French vocabulary that could be used to fill the gaps and complete the sentences.

Then listen to the audio track to hear people talking about the relationships they have with their parents. Fill in the gaps then translate the phrases into English.

1. Mes parents me laissent _____ avec mes _____ tous les week-ends.

2. Mes parents me laissent assez de _____.

3. Mes parents me _____ beaucoup d'argent de _____.

4. Mes parents sont très _____ de ma vie _____.

5. Je _____ très bien avec mes parents car ils me font _____.

6. Mes parents sont très _____ et ils me donnent de bons _____.

7. Je suis très _____ de mes parents car on peut _____ de tout.

8. J'ai de la chance car je _____ de tout avec mes parents et on _____ aux mêmes choses.

9. Ma mère est toujours de bonne _____ et on _____ ensemble.

compréhensifs	donnent	rigole	discuter	conseils	respectueux
liberté	poche	sortir	discute	humeur	confiance
proche	amis	m'entends	s'intéresse	privée	

ONLINE TEST

Take the test 'Relationships – Les relations' at www.brightredbooks.net/N5French.

VIDEO LINK

Check out the clip 'Family and marriage' at www.brightredbooks.net/N5French

THINGS TO DO AND THINK ABOUT

Adapt any phrases that you like about positive family relationships and write a paragraph to describe your relationships with people in your family. You may wish to learn this paragraph for your Performance.

FAMILY CONFLICTS – LES CONFLITS FAMILIAUX 1

Although we may get on well with our families, there can be arguments from time to time. What do you tend to argue about with your parents, brothers and sisters? To introduce family conflicts, you may want to start by saying that you don't get on well with someone in particular and then give reasons why. Here are a few ideas.

 NEGATIVE RELATIONSHIPS 1 – LES RAPPORTS NÉGATIFS 1

Listen to the audio track to hear how these phrases are pronounced then translate them into English.

1. J'ai une mauvaise relation avec ma sœur.
2. J'ai un mauvais rapport avec ma grand-mère.
3. Je m'entends mal avec mon oncle.
4. Je ne m'entends pas bien avec mon frère.
5. Je me dispute souvent avec mes parents.
6. De temps en temps, il y a des tensions avec mes parents.

DON'T FORGET

You can use adverbs of frequency to emphasise how often you argue with your family.

 ADVERBS – LES ADVERBES

Can you work out what these words mean? Use the percentages in brackets as a clue to help you.

1. Toujours (100%)
2. Souvent (70%)
3. Parfois/quelquefois (40%)
4. De temps en temps (30%)
5. Rarement (10%)

Here are some examples of these words in use. Can you work out what the rule is for where to place these **adverbs** of frequency?

1. Je me dispute souvent avec mon frère.
2. On se dispute toujours.
3. Je me dispute parfois avec mon père.
4. On se dispute de temps en temps.
5. Je me dispute rarement avec ma mère.

ONLINE TEST

Take the test 'Family conflicts – Les conflits de la famille' at www.brightredbooks.net/N5French.

  NEGATIVE RELATIONSHIPS 2 – LES RAPPORTS NÉGATIFS 2

Here are some reasons why there may be conflicts or tensions with your family or friends.

Can you work out what they mean?

Je me dispute avec mes parents/mon père/ma mère/mon frère/ma sœur car/parce que/parce qu'…

1. mon père/ma mère/mon frère/ma sœur est + negative adjective.
2. mes parents sont + adjective (*don't forget agreement!*).
3. il/elle est + negative adjective.
4. ils sont + negative adjective (*don't forget agreement!*).
5. il/elle prend mes vêtements sans me demander la permission.

VIDEO LINK

Watch 'Children and their parents' at www.brightredbooks.net/N5French

 contd

6. il/elle ment tout le temps.
7. mes parents veulent regarder des émissions différentes à la télé.
8. il/elle écoute de la musique trop fort quand je fais mes devoirs.
9. il/elle change son comportement devant mes parents.
10. mon père se moque de moi devant mes amis.
11. mes frères me taquinent tout le temps.
12. ma sœur utilise mon maquillage/mon ordinateur sans me demander la permission.

ARGUMENTS - LES DISPUTES

You might want to be more specific about the arguments that you have with your parents. You can start by talking about general reasons for arguments and then go into more detail. When talking about arguments with your parents, make sure you use the third person plural endings (ils).

THINGS TO DO AND THINK ABOUT

Read the following sentences and work out what they mean. Try to find links between English and French vocabulary to help you work out what the vocabulary means before checking in the dictionary.

Listen to the phrases online to help you with pronunciation.

Je me dispute avec mes parents à cause ...

... des études
- Ils pensent que je n'étudie pas assez.
- Ils ne sont pas contents de mes notes au lycée.

... des sorties
- Ils ne me laissent pas sortir avec mes amis pendant la semaine.
- Ils ne me laissent pas assez de liberté.

... de mes amis
... de mon petit ami/ma petite amie
- Ils n'aiment pas mes amis/mon petit ami/ma petite amie.
- Ils pensent que je passe trop de temps avec mes amis.
- Ils croient que je suis trop jeune pour avoir un petit ami/une petite amie.

... de l'argent
- Ils ne me donnent pas assez d'argent.
- Ils pensent que je gaspille mon argent.
- Ils ne me laissent pas trouver un petit boulot pour gagner de l'argent.

... des tâches ménagères
- Ils pensent que je ne fais rien à la maison et que je suis trop paresseux (-euse).
- Je crois que j'aide beaucoup à la maison mais ils ne sont pas d'accord.
- Je dois faire beaucoup de ménage mais mon frère ne fait rien.

... ma vie privée
- Ils se mêlent de mes affaires.
- Ils ne respectent pas ma vie privée.
- Ils veulent toujours savoir ce qui se passe dans ma vie, ce qui m'énerve.
- Ils posent trop de questions de mes amis/de mon petit copain/de ma petite copine/de mes études.

... de mon comportement
- Ils pensent que je suis désobéissant(e).
- Ils ne sont pas contents de mon comportement à la maison/l'école.

... de mes passe-temps
- Ils pensent que je passe trop de temps à regarder la télé/écouter de la musique/jouer à l'ordinateur.

- Ils disent que je passe trop de temps sur internet/sur mon portable/sur Facebook.

FAMILY CONFLICTS– LES CONFLITS FAMILIAUX 2

 **ACTIVITY** ARGUMENTS WITH PARENTS 1 – LES DISPUTES AVEC SES PARENTS 1

Read the following texts about why some young people argue with their parents. Try to identify some of the vocabulary we have already covered.

For each text take notes on the following:

1. Who do they not get on with/argue with?

2. Why?

Jérôme

Malheureusement, je dirais que j'ai une mauvaise relation avec mon père. Il est toujours sur mon dos. Ça m'arrive de me disputer assez souvent avec lui. Il n'est jamais content car il pense que je passe trop de temps sur mon portable. Ce qu'il ne comprend pas, c'est que je veux parler à ma petite amie et le problème, c'est qu'il n'aime pas ma petite amie. Il croit que je suis trop jeune pour avoir une petite amie et que je devrais passer plus de temps à étudier. Ce qui m'énerve, c'est qu'il se mêle de mes affaires et à mon avis, il doit respecter ma vie privée.

Marianne

Parfois il y a des conflits chez moi à cause des tâches ménagères et de l'argent de poche. Ma mère me critique tout le temps et elle me gronde si je ne fais pas la vaisselle ou si je ne passe pas l'aspirateur. Après avoir passé une longue journée au lycée, je n'ai pas envie de faire le ménage. Ce n'est pas juste car mon frère ne fait rien à la maison. En plus, tous mes amis reçoivent vingt Euros chaque semaine de leurs parents sans aider chez eux. Ma mère ne me donnerait rien si je ne faisais pas le ménage, ce que je trouve embêtant. Je ne reçois que dix Euros chaque semaine et ça ne me suffit pas.

Put your answers into the table:

	Jérôme	Marianne
Who does he/she argue with?		
Why?		

 **ACTIVITY:** ARGUMENTS WITH PARENTS 2 –
LES DISPUTES AVEC SES PARENTS 2

Now try to put together some sentences about the arguments you have with your parents.

Here are some 'starters':

- Ça m'arrive souvent de me disputer avec mes parents à cause de … – I often argue with my parents about …

- Il y a des tensions avec mes parents à cause de … – There are tensions with my parents because of …

- À l'égard des conflits chez moi, il y a des disputes à cause de … – With regards to conflicts at home, there are arguments about …

- Ce qui m'énerve, c'est qu'il y a des conflits chez moi à cause de … – What annoys me is that there are conflicts at home because of …

- Ce que je déteste, ce sont les tensions chez moi à cause de … – What I hate are the tensions at home because of …

- Je dirais qu'il y a souvent des conflits chez moi à cause de … – I would say that there are often arguments at home because of …

 DON'T FORGET

Remember, you can adapt and use these phrases in your Performance about your family relationships.

 ONLINE TEST

Take the test 'Family conflicts – Les conflits familiaux' at www. brightredbooks.net/N5French

 VIDEO LINK

For more, watch the clip 'La famille' at www. brightredbooks.net/N5French

 THINGS TO DO AND THINK ABOUT

Write a paragraph about any arguments or tensions in your family. You may wish to use this as part of your Performance.

IDEAL PARENTS – LES PARENTS IDÉAUX

We have talked about reasons why you don't get along with your parents. We will now look at how you would describe your ideal parents. You can recycle some of the language we have already learned in this unit. You will also need to know the **conditional tense**.

- What would be your idea of a perfect parent? What would they be like?
- What would they do and what would they not do?

CONDITIONAL TENSE – LE CONDITIONNEL

You will need to know the conditional tense in order to describe your ideal parents. The conditional tense describes what someone *would* be like or what they *would* do. It is really easy to form as the endings remain the same for 'er', 'ir' and 're' verbs, although there are some irregular conditional stems that you will need to learn.

1. First write down the subject (person who is doing the verb): *Je.*

2. Then write down the infinitive: *Je jouer.*

3. Now add the conditional endings to the infinitive *Je jouerais* – I would play (although take off the 'e' at the end of 're' verbs before adding the endings, e.g. *Je prendrais* – I would take.)

The conditional endings are:

je	-ais	nous	-ions
tu	-ais	vous	-iez
il/elle/on	-ait	ils/elles	-aient

The key irregular conditional verbs that you need to know include:

- avoir – j'aurais (I would have)
- être – je serais (I would be)
- faire – je ferais (I would do/make)
- aller – j'irais (I would go)
- vouloir – je voudrais (I would like)
- pouvoir – je pourrais (I would be able to/could)
- devoir – je devrais (I would have to/should)

 CONDITIONAL TENSE – LE CONDITIONNEL

Try to translate the following sentences using the conditional tense:

1. I would watch TV with my dad.

2. I would finish my homework.

3. I would read a book.

4. We would spend more time together.

5. We would talk more often.

ACTIVITY: IRREGULAR CONDITIONAL STEMS – LES VERBES IRRÉGULIERS AU CONDITIONNEL

Translate the following sentences into French using irregular conditional verbs:

1. I would go to the cinema at the weekend with my mum.
2. My dad would be more patient.
3. My parents would have more free time.
4. I would do sport with my dad.
5. I would be able to go out with my friends during the week.

AN IDEAL PARENT – UN PARENT IDÉAL

Let's start by describing the qualities of an ideal parent: we could use some negatives here as well. Have a look back at the section on negatives (page 8) if you need to revise them again.

ACTIVITY: AN IDEAL PARENT 1 – UN PARENT IDÉAL 1

Listen to the audio track and read the following phrases. Put the phrases in the correct order and translate them into English.

1. Un parent idéal laisserait assez de liberté à ses enfants.
2. Un parent idéal ne s'énerverait pas facilement.
3. Un parent idéal protègerait ses enfants.
4. Un parent idéal ne serait pas trop protecteur.
5. Un parent idéal serait patient et tolérant.
6. Un parent idéal ne serait pas démodé.
7. Un parent idéal serait toujours disponible pour aider ses enfants.
8. Un parent idéal passerait beaucoup de temps avec ses enfants.
9. Un parent idéal donnerait de bons conseils à ses enfants.
10. Un parent idéal ne gâterait jamais ses enfants.
11. Un parent idéal ferait confiance à ses enfants.

ACTIVITY: AN IDEAL PARENT 2 – UN PARENT IDÉAL 2

Now it's your turn. Choose five phrases that describe positive relationships and five phrases that describe negative relationships with parents and change them into the conditional tense to describe an ideal parent. A couple of examples have been done for you:

1. Il/elle a un bon sens de l'humour – Un parent idéal aurait un bon sens de l'humour.
2. Il/elle se moque de moi devant mes amis – Un parent idéal ne se moquerait pas de ses enfants.

THINGS TO DO AND THINK ABOUT

Write a paragraph about an ideal parent/ideal parents. You may wish to learn this as part of your Performance.

ONLINE TEST

Take the test 'Ideal parents – Les parents idéaux' at www.brightredbooks.net/N5French

VIDEO LINK

Watch 'Family and children' at www.brightredbooks.net/N5French

FRIENDSHIP – L'AMITIÉ

Although we have touched on friendship already and some of the phrases we have learned can be used to describe your friendships, we are now going to focus on how you spend time with your friends and peer pressure.

 **ACTIVITY** SPENDING TIME WITH YOUR FAMILY/ FRIENDS – PASSER DU TEMPS AVEC SA FAMILLE/SES AMIS

Listen to the following conversation between two people discussing their friends. Fill in the gaps using the words in the box below. Before listening to the audio track, read through the text and predict what you might hear.

A: J'ai de la chance car ma _____ amie et moi, nous avons les mêmes _____.
On s'amuse bien à faire les _____ le samedi après-midi et le samedi soir, on _____ bien quand nous allons au cinéma. On adore regarder les films _____.
Et toi, Jean-Claude, est-ce tu passes beaucoup de temps avec tes amis?

B: Ah oui. On passe des heures ensemble à jouer au foot car on fait _____ du même club de foot. Ce que _____ le plus c'est participer aux matchs de foot le _____ matin avec mes amis.

A: Est-ce que tu as un meilleur ami?

B: Oui, il s'appelle Philippe et il est _____ et vraiment sympa. On _____ aux mêmes sports, donc on regarde les sports à la _____. Je peux compter sur lui et si j'ai un problème, il _____ et il me donne de bons _____.

A: Selon moi, le plus important c'est qu'on est sur la même _____ _____. J'aime bien discuter de tout avec ma meilleure amie et je peux lui faire _____.

drôle	magasins	m'aide	rigole	j'aime	meilleure	s'intéresse	conseils
samedi	confiance	comiques	intérêts	télé	partie	longueur d'onde	

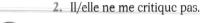 **ACTIVITY** RELATIONSHIPS WITH FRIENDS – LES RAPPORTS AVEC SES AMIS

Read the following phrases and decide if the phrases are describing a good friend or a bad friend. Listen to the audio track to help with pronunciation. You might want to practise translating the phrases into English.

1. Il/elle me comprend.
2. Il/elle ne me critique pas.
3. Il/elle m'encourage rarement.
4. Il/elle ne me soutient jamais.
5. Il/elle m'énerve.
6. Il/elle n'est pas embêtant(e).
7. Il/elle n'est jamais jaloux(-se).
8. Il/elle m'ennuie.
9. Il/elle a le sens de l'humour.
10. Il/elle se plaint tout le temps.
11. Il/elle n'est pas égoïste.
12. Il/elle me respecte.
13. Il/elle ne m'écoute jamais.
14. Je peux me confier à lui/elle.
15. Il/elle m'ignore à l'école.
16. Il/elle est toujours là quand j'ai besoin de quelqu'un.
17. Il/elle se dispute pour n'importe quoi.

ACTIVITY: TRANSLATING THE CONDITIONAL TENSE

Put the phrases above into the conditional tense to describe what a good friend *would* do, then translate them into English. You might need to turn some phrases into negative sentences (refer back to the notes on negatives on page 8).

Here are a few to start you off:

1. Un bon ami me comprend**rait**.

2. Un bon ami **ne me** **critiquerait pas**.

3. Il/elle m'encourage**rait**.

Write a paragraph about your friends. You might want to include what makes a good friend and how you spend time with your friends. You may wish to use this as part of your Performance.

ACTIVITY: PEER PRESSURE – L'INFLUENCE DES PAIRS

When we are talking about friendship, peer pressure often arises as a topic for discussion. Read the following phrases and decide if the person in each sentence is influenced by his/her peers or not.

1. J'aime me sentir à l'aise avec mes amis donc je fais comme mes amis.

2. Je fais ce que je veux sans m'inquiéter des avis des autres jeunes.

3. Je me sens le mieux quand je suis au sein d'un groupe d'amis.

4. J'ai peur des opinions et du jugement des autres.

5. J'ai envie d'être original et différent de mes amis.

6. Je ne veux pas me sentir isolé(e) ou seul(e).

7. J'ai l'habitude de m'habiller comme mes amis.

8. J'ai de la chance car je ne fais pas attention à ce que mes amis pensent.

9. Ce que j'aime le plus, c'est qu'on porte ce qu'on veut.

10. J'ai du mal à montrer ma personnalité à mes amis.

11. J'ai envie de m'intégrer à une bande donc je dois être comme les autres.

12. J'ai besoin d'acheter les vêtements de marques.

13. J'ai l'occasion de sortir avec mes amis tous les week-ends et je ne voudrais pas être exclu(e).

14. J'ai de la chance car mes amis ne me jugent jamais.

15. Je fume comme tous mes amis afin d'avoir l'air cool.

16. Je dois toujours suivre mes amis, ce qui m'énerve de temps en temps.

17. J'ai de la chance car je peux m'identifier à mes amis et on n'est pas obligé d'avoir les mêmes goûts.

18. Je trouve ça difficile de résister à l'influence des pairs car je ne veux pas être différent(e).

ONLINE TEST
Take the test 'Friendship – L'amitié' at www. brightredbooks.net/N5French

ONLINE
Check out the link 'Conditional tense' at www. brightredbooks.net/N5French

DON'T FORGET
Ce que and *ce qui* are called **relative pronouns**. You will notice *ce qui* and *ce que* in these phrases. Can you work out what they mean?

THINGS TO DO AND THINK ABOUT

From the sentences about peer pressure, can you pick out any **avoir phrases**? Here is a list of some useful avoir phrases. Do you know what they mean?

- Avoir besoin de
- Avoir envie de
- Avoir peur de
- Avoir l'occasion de
- Avoir de la chance de
- Avoir du mal à
- Avoir l'air
- Avoir soif
- Avoir faim
- Avoir chaud
- Avoir froid

Can you make up a sentence using each of these avoir phrases?

PEOPLE WHO INFLUENCE ME – LES GENS QUI M'INFLUENCENT

PHRASES THAT EXPRESS WHO INFLUENCES YOU AND WHY

If you are asked who influences you, you might think of a member of your family. Here are some phrases to express who influences you and why.

- Ma famille m'inspire – My family inspires me
- Ma famille m'influence, chacun à leur façon – My family influence me, each in their own way
- Mon frère joue un rôle très important dans ma vie – My brother plays a very important role in my life
- Je trouve que ma mère m'influence beaucoup – I find that my mum influences me a lot
- La personne qui m'influence le plus, c'est mon père – The person who influences me the most is my dad
- Mes parents peuvent influencer mes choix– My parents can influence my choices
- Une personne qui m'influence dans ma vie est mon grand-père – One person who influences me in life is my grandfather
- Mon (ma) meilleur(e) ami(e) influence mes décisions – My best friend influences my decisions

Here are some reasons why:

- ... car il/elle est sage – because he/she is wise
- ... car je passe la plupart de mon temps libre avec lui/elle – because I spend most of my free time with him/her
- ... car je le/la respecte – because I respect him/her
- ... car il/elle me donne de bons conseils– because he/she gives me good advice
- ... car il/elle a toujours raison – because he/she is always right

![Two men looking under the bonnet of a car]

 ACTIVITY PEER PRESSURE AND INFLUENCE -

Write a paragraph about whether or not you feel peer pressure and about the people who influence you. Again, this could be used as part of your Performance.

RELATIONSHIPS WITH FAMILY AND FRIENDS: RECAP

By the end of this section, you should have written various paragraphs on the following topics:

Who is in your family: personal information (name, age, description)

What they are like: physical description, personal qualities (positive and negative)

Your relationship with them: why you get on well, what you do together

Any conflicts there might be: the reasons for arguments

Ideal relationships: ideal parents, ideal brothers and sisters, ideal friendships

Influences: peer pressure, other people who influence you

You should also feel confident about the following grammar points:

- present tense of regular and irregular verbs
- adjective agreements
- negatives
- conditional tense
- avoir phrases.

Test yourself: Vocabulary

Can you recall and write down:

- three positive adjectives?
- three negative adjectives?
- three positive phrases about your relationship with your family?
- three negative phrases about your relationship with your family?
- three phrases about ideal parents?
- three phrases about what you do with your friends/family?
- three phrases about peer pressure?

Test yourself: Knowledge about language

Can you recall:

- the rule about adjective agreements?
- six negatives?
- how to form the present tense?
- how to form the conditional tense?
- three avoir phrases?
- three adverbs of frequency?
- what *ce qui* and *ce que* mean?

THINGS TO DO AND THINK ABOUT

You have learned a lot in this section and used your listening, reading, dictionary and writing skills, as well as learning vocabulary and grammar rules. Following the 'Test yourself' tasks, is there any area that you are not sure of? If so, look over this section again and revise the vocabulary or grammar that is causing you difficulty.

LEISURE – LES LOISIRS 1

You will know quite a lot of vocabulary already about *les loisirs*, like different types of sports and hobbies. When thinking about your hobbies, you could mention the following:

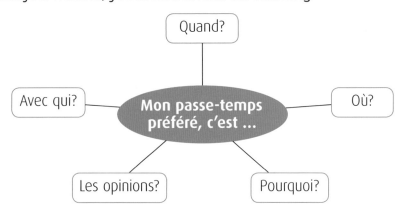

VIDEO LINK

Check out the clip 'Leisure activities in the country' at www.brightredbooks.net/N5French

VIDEO LINK

Have a look at the clip 'Les loisirs – la musique' at www.brightredbooks.net/N5French

ACTIVITY: REVISION – LA RÉVISION

It is useful to be able to say how often you do your hobbies, when, with whom, why and where, which you could include in a piece of writing or as part of your Performance.

Here are a few phrases to start you off. Can you work out what they mean?

Mon passe-temps préféré, c'est ...

- jouer au tennis
- faire de la natation
- la lecture
- aller au cinéma
- faire du shopping
- regarder la télé
- faire de l'équitation
- faire les magasins.

VIDEO LINK

Watch the clip 'Avec la famille' to hear children talking about what they do with their family, at www.brightredbooks.net/N5French

Avec qui?

- Avec mes amis/mes copains
- Avec mon père/ma mère
- Je suis membre d'un club
- Je fais partie d'une équipe
- Tout(e) seul(e)

Quand?

- Le samedi matin
- Le mardi après les cours
- Le mercredi soir
- Le dimanche après-midi
- Une fois par semaine
- Trois fois par mois
- Souvent
- Quelquefois
- De temps en temps
- Rarement

contd

Où?

- Au parc
- Au centre-ville
- Au centre sportif
- Au terrain de foot/golf
- Chez moi
- Dans le jardin

Les opinions?

- J'adore ...
- J'aime ...
- Je me passionne
- Je m'intéresse

Pourquoi?

- C'est amusant
- C'est passionnant
- C'est divertissant
- C'est relaxant
- Je peux rencontrer de nouvelles personnes
- Ça m'aide à me détendre
- C'est un bon moyen de s'échapper du stress de la vie scolaire
- C'est bon pour la santé
- Ça me tient en bonne forme

DON'T FORGET

Look at the section on healthy living to find more reasons for why you do your hobbies.

 ACTIVITY: HOBBIES – LES PASSE-TEMPS

The following list is a reminder of some of the more difficult vocabulary to do with hobbies. Can you remember what the following words/phrases mean? If not, look up any unfamiliar vocabulary in the dictionary.

- Faire du cheval
- Faire du shopping
- Faire du vélo
- Faire du VTT
- Faire de l'escalade
- Faire de la voile
- Faire de la planche à voile
- Faire de la plongée
- Faire de la randonnée
- Faire des sports aquatiques
- Faire les courses/les magasins
- Faire une promenade
- Faire une balade à vélo/à bateau
- Nager
- Lire des romans
- Sortir avec mes amis
- Passer du temps avec mes amis
- Aller à une fête/en boîte/à une soirée
- Aller au cinéma/au théâtre
- Aller à la piscine
- Regarder la télé/les films
- Ecouter de la musique sur mon iPod
- Passer des heures sur Internet/sur Facebook
- Bavarder avec mes amis sur mon portable
- Rendre visite à quelqu'un

DON'T FORGET

Some of these phrases are translated into English with a different verb, for example *faire une promenade* means 'to go for a walk'.

 THINGS TO DO AND THINK ABOUT

Don't forget to revise "les verbes irréguliers"!

To describe what you do during your free time, you need to know verbs in the present tense. Refer to page 7 to revise how to form the present tense and 'er', 'ir' and 're' verb endings.

ONLINE TEST

Why not try the 'Irregular verbs' online test to revise these, including aller and faire, at www.brightredbooks.net/N5French.

LEISURE – LES LOISIRS 2

TO DO SPORT – FAIRE DU SPORT

To say which sports and hobbies you do, you need to know the verb faire.

If the sport or hobby:

- is masculine, then faire is followed by *du*, for example *le judo – faire du judo*
- is feminine, then faire is followed by *de la*, for example *la natation – faire de la natation*
- begins with a vowel or a silent 'h', faire is followed by *de l'*, for example *l'athlétisme – faire de l'athlétisme*
- is plural, then faire is followed by *des*, for example *les sports aquatiques – faire des sports aquatiques.*

VIDEO LINK

Watch the clip 'Sport and leisure activities in Marseille' at www.brightredbooks.net/N5French

⚙ ACTIVITY TO DO SPORT – FAIRE DU SPORT

Translate the following sentences into French using the correct part of faire and *du, de la, de l'* or *des*.

1. I go cycling.
2. He goes mountain biking.
3. She goes swimming.
4. We go hiking.
5. They (masculine) go horse-riding.
6. I go windsurfing.
7. You (formal) go sailing.
8. They (feminine) do water sports.

VIDEO LINK

Check out the clip 'Le sport' to hear about different sports which are practiced in Sénégal at www.brightredbooks.net/N5French

TO GO TO THE TOWN CENTRE – ALLER AU CENTRE-VILLE

Aller is another very important irregular verb that you need to know. There are different ways of saying 'to the' in French, depending on whether the place:

- is masculine, for example *le parc –Je vais au parc*
- is feminine, for example *la piscine – Je vais à la piscine*
- begins with a vowel or silent h, for example *l'école – Je vais à l'école*
- is plural, for example *les magasins – Je vais aux magasins.*

 ACTIVITY: TO GO TO THE ... – ALLER AU/À LA/À L'/AUX ...

Translate the following sentences into French using the correct part of aller and *au, à la, à l'* or *aux*.

1. I am going to the cinema.

2. He is going to the sports centre.

3. She is going to the beach.

4. We are going to the shops.

5. They (masculine) are going to the theatre.

6. I am going to the shopping centre.

7. You (formal) are going to the restaurant.

8. They (feminine) are going to the hotel.

 ##  ACTIVITY: OPINIONS – LES OPINIONS

It is a good idea to revise opinion phrases in more detail at this stage. Read and listen to the following passage and pick out all the opinion phrases. You may wish to try to include them in your writing and Performance.

Jacques

Je crois que je suis très sportif. J'adore passer mon temps libre à faire du sport. Mon sport préféré, c'est le basket. Ce que j'aime le plus, c'est jouer au basket avec mes amis car on s'amuse bien à jouer en équipe. Je pense que ma sœur n'aime pas le basket. Elle préfère nager car elle dit que c'est bon pour la santé. Elle s'entraîne trois fois par semaine et elle adore ça. En ce qui me concerne, j'ai horreur de la natation car ça me fatigue et je trouve ça ennuyeux. Mon père s'intéresse au sport aussi et on passe des heures à regarder le sport à la télé. Il croit que ça aide à se détendre après avoir passé la journée au travail. Ma mère déteste le sport à la télé. Elle préfère regarder des films romantiques, ce que je trouve barbant. En effet, elle préférerait passer des heures à lire un bon roman au lieu de regarder la télé. Elle pense que c'est un bon moyen d'échapper à la vie de tous les jours.

As well as picking out the key opinion phrases, can you note down what each person enjoys doing in their free time and why?

 ## THINGS TO DO AND THINK ABOUT

You should revise other sports and hobbies, opinions and adverbs of time in French at this stage to refresh your memory. Write a paragraph on how you spend your free time and try to include some of the fancier phrases. Include when you do these hobbies, how often, where and with whom. You might also want to refer to the section on using technology and the internet in your free time (refer to pages 38–9). This paragraph can be used as a piece of writing and also as part of your Performance.

 VIDEO LINK

For a great clip about what leisure activities people get up to at the weekend, watch the clip 'Les loisirs – le weekend' at www.brightredbooks.net/N5French

 ONLINE TEST

Try the 'Leisure – Les loisirs' test online at www.brightredbooks.net/N5French

 DON'T FORGET

If you are unsure about whether a verb is regular or irregular, check the verb section in your bilingual dictionary. This section will also give you examples of the verb formed in different tenses.

HEALTHY LIFESTYLE – LA VIE SAINE 1

In this section you will learn to talk about what you do to stay healthy. We will divide it into what physical exercise we do and what we eat and drink to keep healthy.

USEFUL VOCABULARY

Here is some useful vocabulary that will help you to describe how to stay healthy. Spend a few minutes looking at this vocabulary and then cover up the English meanings. How many of these words you can remember? Revise the ones that you are having difficulty with and then cover the English again to see if you can remember them all. Leave it for a while and then come back to this vocabulary. How many can you remember now?

il faut + infinitive	it is necessary to/you must
il ne faut pas + infinitive	it is not necessary to/you must not
on doit + infinitive	we must
on ne doit pas + infinitive	we must not
boire de l'eau	to drink water
contrôler le stress	to control stress
dormir	to sleep
être en bonne santé	to be in good health
faire de l'exercice	to do exercise
faire attention à sa santé	to take care of your health
faire du sport	to do sport
manger cinq portions de fruits ou légumes par jour	to eat five portions of fruit and vegetables per day
manger de la nourriture fraîche	to eat fresh food
mener une vie active	to lead an active life
rester en bonne forme	to stay fit
suivre un régime sain	to follow a healthy diet
suivre un régime équilibré	to follow a balanced diet
trouver l'équilibre entre le travail et les loisirs	to find the balance between work and leisure
boire des boissons gazeuses	to drink fizzy drinks
éviter les sucreries	to avoid sweet things
éviter les matières grasses	to avoid fatty foods
prendre du poids/grossir	to put on weight

DON'T FORGET

Il faut means 'it is necessary to' or 'you must' and can be used in lots of different contexts. It is followed by the infinitive.

DON'T FORGET

On doit is part of the verb *devoir*. Devoir belongs to an important group of irregular verbs called modal verbs.

ONLINE

Take the 'Using modal verbs' test online at www. brightredbooks.net/N5French

VIDEO LINK

Watch the clip 'Healthy living and fitness' at www. brightredbooks.net/N5French

MODAL VERBS

A **modal verb** is a verb associated with possibility or necessity, such as can, could, may, might, must, shall, should, will and would. In French, the modal verbs are:

vouloir – to want to
Je veux jouer au foot – I want to play football
Je voudrais jouer au foot – I would like to play football

devoir – to have to/must
Je dois manger sainement – I have to/must eat healthily
On devrait manger sain – We should eat healthily

pouvoir – to be able to/can
Je peux faire du sport – I am able to/can do sport
On pourrait manger plus de légumes – We could eat more vegetables

contd

savoir – to know how to
Je sais manger sainement – I know how to eat healthily
On sait mener une vie active – We know how to lead an active life

ACTIVITY: HEALTHY LIVING

Read the following texts and answer the questions in English. Here are some tips for how to approach a reading comprehension for the Course and Unit reading assessments.

- You might want to read the questions first before skimming over the passage in French. This will give you an idea of what the text is about before you even begin to read the French.
- You might want to think about the type of vocabulary you are looking for in the text, for example if the question asks you when something happens, you will need to think about time phrases.
- Looking at the number of marks given for each answer will indicate how much information you need to look for.
- When you skim the text, find the parts of the passage that answer the questions by spotting key words.
- Then take each question at a time and read the text more closely, looking up any unfamiliar vocabulary in the dictionary.

Pierre

En ce qui concerne la santé, il est important de manger équilibré pour satisfaire nos besoins nutritionnels. Il faut varier l'alimentation et éviter les matières grasses et sucrées comme les pizzas, les frites, les chips et le chocolat car si on mange des aliments trop gras et trop sucrés, on peut devenir obèse. L'obésité peut mener à des maladies comme le diabète ou les maladies du cœur. Si on mange de la viande et du poisson, on a une source de protéines et de fer. Comme source de fibre, de vitamines et de minéraux, il faut manger des fruits et des légumes. En plus, les produits laitiers, comme le lait et le fromage, apportent du calcium, ce qui est important pour le corps. Je dirais que l'eau est essentielle pour l'hydratation et il faut boire au moins deux litres d'eau par jour. Par contre, il faut éviter de boire trop de caféine et d'alcool afin de rester en bonne santé. Finalement, je pense qu'il faut prendre l'habitude de manger de tout, en quantité raisonnable.

1. Why does Pierre think eating a balanced diet is important? (1)
2. What does he think you should avoid and why? (2)
3. What can obesity lead to? (2)
4. What do meat and fish provide us with? (2)
5. What should we eat in order to have fibre, vitamins and minerals? (2)
6. Which two examples of dairy products does Pierre mention? (2)
7. What does Pierre say about water? (2)
8. What does he think you should avoid drinking? (2)

Thérèse

A l'égard de la santé, je sais qu'il est nécessaire de manger une alimentation équilibrée et saine. Pour ma part, j'aime bien manger des matières grasses et des sucreries comme le chocolat et les bonbons. En plus j'adore boire des boissons gazeuses même si je sais qu'elles contiennent beaucoup de sucre. C'est vrai que je grignotte beaucoup pour me consoler car cette année il y a beaucoup de pression à l'école. Donc je prends du poids et je me sens déprimée. Pour perdre du poids, j'ai commencé à sauter les repas mais je sais que ce n'est pas une bonne idée. Je dors mal et pendant les cours au lycée, je ne peux pas me concentrer à cause de cette perte de sommeil et de cette fatigue. Je mange au McDo avec mes amis deux fois par semaine et, à mon avis, c'est génial car le service est rapide et ce n'est pas cher. Ma mère dit que le fast-food n'est pas bon pour la santé. Elle a horreur des produits gras comme les hamburgers et les frites car ils contiennent trop de calories.

1. What does Thérèse like to eat? (2)
2. What does she like to drink? (1)
3. Why does Thérèse eat so many snacks? (2)
4. What has caused Thérèse to feel depressed? (1)
5. What has she started doing to lose weight? (1)
6. Thérèse finds it difficult to sleep. What problem is this causing? (1)
7. Why does Thérèse like McDonalds? (2)
8. Give two reasons why Thérèse's mum does not approve of fast-food restaurants. (2)

THINGS TO DO AND THINK ABOUT

If there are any useful phrases about what to eat and drink to stay healthy and what to avoid, take a note of these and learn them so you may wish to use them in your Performance.

HEALTHY LIFESTYLE – LA VIE SAINE 2

Now we will look at other ways of staying healthy and focus on doing physical exercise and keeping fit.

 ACTIVITY KEEPING FIT

Listen to three people talking about what they do to keep fit. Fill in the blanks using the vocabulary in the boxes below each section. Read through the text first and try to predict what you might hear. Use the dictionary to look up any unfamiliar vocabulary.

Alain

Pour être en forme, il faut faire régulièrement de _____ _____ et suivre un régime _____ sain. J'aime bien le tennis et j'y joue _____ cinq ans. Je suis très _____ et je m'amuse bien quand je joue au tennis avec mes amis. Quand j'étais plus jeune, j'ai joué au golf avec mon père. En été, j'ai passe des heures au _____. Je trouve que maintenant j'ai trop de devoirs à faire donc je n'ai pas assez du temps pour _____ au golf et au tennis. J'ai dû choisir entre les deux sports et comme aucun de mes amis ne joue au golf, j'ai décidé de _____ à jouer au tennis. Je ne passe pas beaucoup de temps devant _____, comme la télé ou l'ordinateur parce que je me rends compte que si on veut _____ la forme, on doit faire de l'exercice physique.

l'exercice physique   jouer   continuer   alimentaire   depuis   les écrans   garder
compétitif   terrain de golf   aérobic

Brigitte

Je dois admettre que je ne suis pas très _____. Je n'aime pas vraiment le sport et je préfère lire un bon livre ou regarder un film au ciné puisque ça __ _____. Je n'ai pas la motivation pour aller au _____ ou pour faire du sport. Au lycée, je joue au _____ pendant les cours d'EPS. C'est rigolo mais très fatigant. Pour rester en bonne santé, je vais au lycée __ _____ au lieu de prendre le bus. En plus, je monte _____ à pied au lieu de prendre l' _____. Je sais qu'un manque d'activité physique peut être à l'origine des _____. Quand je serai plus grande, je n'ai pas envie de devenir _____. Par conséquent, après avoir quitté le lycée, j'ai _____ de faire plus d'exercice physique.

gymnase   active   me détend   obèse   ascenseur   basket   maladies   à pied
l'escalier   l'intention

Antoine

Ce que j'aime le plus, c'est la _____. Je suis membre d'un club et je vais à _____ quatre fois par semaine. La semaine dernière j'ai participé à un _____ de natation. Je n'ai pas gagné mais _____ amusant car j'ai des amis qui font partie du même club de natation. L'entraînement commence à six heures le matin donc avant d'aller au lycée je dois __ _____ tôt et aller à la _____. Il est important de __ _____ assez tôt aussi, toujours avant 22 heures. Je trouve que la natation m'aide à contrôler le stress et à mon avis, il faut trouver _____ entre le travail au lycée et les loisirs. J'ai de la chance car je ne suis pas souvent _____ grâce à ma vie active et saine.

malade   concours   natation   piscine   me lever   l'entraînement   c'était
me coucher   l'équilibre

KNOWLEDGE ABOUT LANGUAGE

In the listening texts, you heard phrases in the **perfect tense** (*j'ai joué*), the **simple future** tense (*je serai*) and the **imperfect tense** (*c'*était). To revise the perfect and imperfect tenses, see pages 43 and 67–9.

The simple future – Le futur simple

The simple future tense is used to describe an action that *will* happen in the future. It is similar to the conditional tense in how it is formed:

1. First write down the subject (person who is doing the verb): *Je*.
2. Then write down the infinitive: *Je jouer*.
3. Now add the simple future endings to the infinitive: *Je jouerai* – I will play (although take off the 'e' at the end of 're' verbs before adding the endings, e.g. *Je prendrai* – I will take).

The simple future endings are:

je	-ai	nous	-ons
tu	-as	vous	-ez
il/elle/on	-a	ils/elles	-ont

 **ACTIVITY:** THE SIMPLE FUTURE – LE FUTUR SIMPLE

Now translate the following sentences using the simple future tense:

1. I will spend less time watching TV.
2. I will eat healthily.
3. I will play football with my friends.
4. We will drink two litres of water per day.
5. We will avoid fatty foods.

IRREGULAR FUTURE STEMS

The key irregular future stems that you need to know include:

- avoir – j'aurai (I will have)
- être – je serai (I will be)
- faire – je ferai (I will do/make)
- aller – j'irai (I will go)
- vouloir – je voudrai (I will like)
- pouvoir – je pourrai (I will be able to/could)
- devoir – je devrai (I will have to/should).

 **ACTIVITY:** IRREGULAR VERBS IN THE SIMPLE FUTURE TENSE – LES IRRÉGULIERS AU FUTUR SIMPLE

Translate the following sentences into French using the irregular conditional stems:

1. I will go to the gym.
2. I will do more sport.
3. I will have to do more physical exercise.
4. We will be able to stay fit.
5. We will be more active.

 THINGS TO DO AND THINK ABOUT

Can you write down ten sentences to do with staying healthy? Try to include phrases about both eating habits and an active lifestyle (including what to avoid in order to stay fit and healthy).

You might also want to include phrases in different tenses. Try to mention the following:

- what you do to keep healthy at the moment (present tense)
- what you used to do (imperfect tense)
- what you will do in future (future tense)
- what you would do if you had more time (conditional tense).

 DON'T FORGET

Se lever and *se coucher* are **reflexive verbs**.

 ONLINE TEST

Take the 'La vie saine' test online at www.brightredbooks.net/N5French

 VIDEO LINK

Watch the clip 'Le sport' at www.brightredbooks.net/N5French

LIFESTYLE-RELATED ILLNESSES – LES MALADIES

We have looked at ways of staying healthy. Now we are going to learn to talk about unhealthy lifestyles. In this section we will look at why people choose to smoke, drink alcohol or take drugs and what the consequences are.

BRAINSTORMING VOCABULARY

There are many illnesses that are caused by unhealthy lifestyles. Can you think of any lifestyle choices that could cause different illnesses? Here are some words to help you get started:

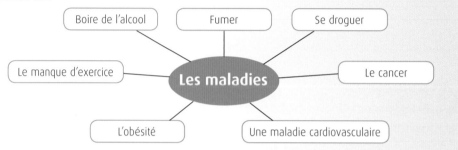

Boire de l'alcool · Fumer · Se droguer · Le manque d'exercice · **Les maladies** · Le cancer · L'obésité · Une maladie cardiovasculaire

GENERAL VOCABULARY

Here is some general vocabulary that is useful to know. Cover the English meanings and 'traffic light' the vocabulary you already know. Then focus on the vocabulary you don't know and learn it.

French	English
le tabagisme	smoking
fumer des cigarettes	to smoke cigarettes
consommer l'alcool	to consume alcohol
essayer l'alcool	to try alcohol
être nuisible à la santé	to be harmful to your health
prendre de la drogue	to take drugs
se droguer	to take drugs
la dépendance	addiction
la toxicomanie	drug addiction

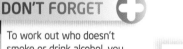 **DON'T FORGET**

To work out who doesn't smoke or drink alcohol, you need to look out for negative words. Look back to page 9 to revise the different negatives in French.

DON'T FORGET

You will notice how *j'ai peur* and *je n'ai pas envie* are used in some sentences. Look back to page 19 to revise avoir phrases.

 **ACTIVITY** SMOKING AND ALCOHOL – LE TABAC ET L'ALCOOL

You might want to think about why people choose to make their lifestyle choices. Read and listen to the phrases below. First, decide if the person talking smokes or drinks alcohol or doesn't smoke or drink alcohol. Then try to work out why, looking up any words you don't know in the dictionary. After translating the phrases into English, choose which ones apply to you and memorise them as these can be used in your Performance.

Listening to the phrases online will help you with the pronunciation.

1. Je ne bois pas d'alcool car ce n'est pas bon pour la santé.
2. Je bois de l'alcool car ça me donne confiance en moi.
3. Je ne fume plus car le tabagisme coûte trop cher.
4. Je bois de l'alcool car j'ai envie d'échapper aux soucis de tous les jours.
5. Je ne fume jamais car c'est nuisible pour la santé.

contd

6. Je ne bois jamais d'alcool car ça a un effet négatif sur le comportement.
7. Je bois de l'alcool car je ne veux pas être différent(e) de mes amis.
8. Je ne bois pas d'alcool car mes parents ne me feraient plus confiance.
9. Je fume car ça m'aide à me relaxer.
10. Je bois de l'alcool car tous mes amis boivent de l'alcool.
11. Je fume car c'est une habitude et c'est mon choix.
12. Je bois de l'alcool car ça m'aide à me sentir plus à l'aise.
13 Je ne fume pas car il y a un risque de dépendance.
14. Je ne bois pas d'alcool car mes parents seraient en colère contre moi.
15. Je fume car je pense qu'on a l'air cool.
16. Même si je suis entouré(e) de personnes qui fument, je n'ai pas envie de fumer car c'est dangereux pour la santé.
17. Tous mes problèmes disparaissent quand je bois de l'alcool.
18. Je ne fume jamais car j'ai peur que je ne pourrais pas m'arrêter.
19. Je fume car ça me détend quand je suis stressé(e).
20. Je ne bois pas d'alcool car je n'aime pas le goût et je ne fume pas car ça sent mauvais.

For an extra activity on lifestyle-related illnesses, head to the BrightRED Digital Zone.

ACTIVITY: WHY DO PEOPLE SMOKE OR DRINK ALCOHOL? – POURQUOI EST-CE QU'ON FUME OU BOIT DE L'ALCOOL?

Listen to the following three people talk about their lifestyles. Fill in the blanks using the words below.

Frédéric

J'ai envie d'être comme mes _____ donc je fume. Tous mes amis _____ des cigarettes alors c'est vrai que je suis toujours entouré de personnes qui fument. Je pense que nous avons _____ cool. C'est mon choix et je suis _____ quand je fume. En effet, je dirais que fumer, ça _____ à me détendre. Je sais qu'il y a des _____ comme le cancer mais je ne veux pas m'arrêter.

> amis   heureux   fument   aide   l'air   risques

Sandrine

Je bois de _____ depuis deux ans. Mes parents me laissent boire _____ de vin de temps en temps. Quand je sors avec mes amis, je bois de l'alcool car ça me donne _____ en moi. Il est vrai que la plupart de mes amis boivent de l'alcool _____ et il y en a qui boivent trop. Ce que je n'aime pas, c'est quand ils sont _____ car l'alcool a un effet très négatif sur le _____, ce qui peut être vraiment gênant.

> confiance   ivres   comportement   l'alcool   un verre   régulièrement

Jean-Luc

Il y a trois semaines, je suis sorti avec mes copains le vendredi soir. Un de mes amis m'a _____ du cannabis mais j'ai refusé d'en prendre. Parfois je bois de l'alcool et je fume mais je n'ai pas envie de prendre de la _____. Je la trouve dangereuse car, en _____, on peut devenir _____. Je sais que si on se drogue, on peut avoir une sensation de peur, de fatigue et une perte du sommeil. Le plus grave c'est que si on prend une _____ de drogue, on peut mourir. En plus, si mes parents savaient que j'avais essayé le cannabis, ils seraient en _____ et ils ne me laisseraient plus de liberté.

> surdose   drogue   colère   essayant   dépendant   offert

VIDEO LINK

Check out 'Le fast food' at www.brightredbooks.net/N5French

ONLINE TEST

Take the test 'Les maladies' at www.brightredbooks.net/N5French

DON'T FORGET

Depuis means 'since' or for' and when used with a present tense verb it means you *have been doing* that verb for a certain length of time, for example *Je joue au foot depuis deux ans* means 'I have been playing football for two years'. *Il y a* usually means 'there is' or 'there are' but when it is followed by a time phrase, it means 'ago', for example *il y a deux semaines* means 'two weeks ago'.

DON'T FORGET

The small word *en* is very useful, it can mean 'of it' or 'of them', depending on the context, e.g. *il y en a* means 'there are some of them'.

THINGS TO DO AND THINK ABOUT

Are there any phrases from these activities that you could use or that you could adapt? Jot down the phrases that apply to you and learn them as you may wish to use them for your Performance.

TELEVISION – LA TÉLÉ

In this section, you will learn to describe what you watch on TV.

USEFUL VOCABULARY

Here is some useful vocabulary to revise what we watch on TV. Match the French vocabulary to the correct image. Try to work out what the French vocabulary means by making links to English vocabulary, for example *une comédie* is 'a comedy' in English.

1. Les informations/les actualités
2. Les documentaires (sur la nature/l'histoire)
3. Les émissions de sport/de musique
4. Les dessins-animés
5. Les feuilletons
6. Un jeu télévisé
7. La publicité
8. La météo
9. Un western
10. Une comédie
11. Un film d'aventure
12. Un film de guerre
13. Un film de science-fiction
14. Un film policier
15. Un film d'espionnage
16. Un drame psychologique
17. Un film d'horreur
18. Un film romantique

(a)

(b)

(c)

(d)

(e)

(f)

contd

(g) (h) (i) (j) (k) (l) (m) (n) (o) (p) (q) (r)

 THINGS TO DO AND THINK ABOUT

Want to see how you did? Get the answers at the back of the book.

 ONLINE TEST

Try the 'False friends' test online at www. brightredbooks.net/N5French

WATCHING TV – REGARDER LA TÉLÉ

As well as saying what you watch on TV, it would be good to be able to say how long you spend watching TV and what you enjoy watching, with reasons for your opinions.

 **ACTIVITY** OPINIONS OF DIFFERENT PROGRAMMES – LES OPINIONS DES ÉMISSIONS DIFFÉRENTES

Listen to the following text and fill in the blanks using the words below. Read the text first and try to predict what you might hear, using the context as a basis for your prediction. Look up any new words in the dictionary before you start.

Sandra

Je passe environ deux heures par jour devant le petit _____. J'aime surtout regarder les _____ et les comédies. Je les trouve _____ et pour moi, c'est un bon moyen de ___ _____ car je ne dois pas trop me concentrer.

écran   me détendre   feuilletons   divertissants

Anna

Je ne passe pas beaucoup de temps à regarder la télé car c'est une _____ de temps. Il y a trop de jeunes qui regardent la télé _____ _____ et ce n'est pas bon pour la santé. Si je regarde la télé, je préfère regarder les _____ et les émissions qui m'instruisent et qui _____.

m'informent   perte   documentaires   sans arrêt

Christophe

Normalement, je n'ai pas assez de temps pour regarder la télé ___ _____ car j'ai trop de devoirs. Le vendredi soir, j'adore regarder les films _____ et les films d'horreur avec mes amis car je les trouve _____. Le samedi soir, ma famille et moi aimons regarder les ____ _____. Je pense qu'ils sont rigolos et quelquefois, il y a des questions difficiles, alors on peut apprendre des choses.

en semaine   passionnants   jeux télévisés   policiers

Simon

Je regarde les informations et ___ _____ à la télé donc je ne passe qu'une heure par jour devant le petit écran. Je crois que la télé est un bon moyen de _____ et de découvrir ce qui se passe dans le _____ entier. Ce qui est bien, c'est qu'on peut voir les images en direct, donc c'est plus _____ que la radio.

communiquer   monde   frappant   la météo

contd

Céline

Je passe la plupart de mon temps libre à regarder la télé. Ma mère dit que je suis
_____ à la télé-réalité. Mon émission préférée s'appelle 'Top Chef' et je ne _____
jamais un épisode. Ma mère pense que c'est une émission superficielle et _____.
Elle m'encourage à faire d'autres choses plus actives car elle a peur que la télé ne me
rende _____.

bête   rate   accro   paresseuse

PRECEDING DIRECT OBJECTS

You will notice *je le trouve, je la trouve* and *je les trouve* appear in some of the reading and listening texts. In these phrases *le, la* and *les* are known as **preceding direct objects**. Can you guess what they mean from the contexts?

Look at the examples and their translations and work out the grammar rule:

a. J'adore le sport. Je le regarde à la télé tous les jours.
   I love sport. I watch it on TV every day.

b. J'adore ma jupe. Je la porte souvent.
   I love my skirt. I often wear it.

c. Je n'aime pas mes voisins, je les déteste!
   I don't like my neighbours, I hate them!

Le and *la* are translated as 'it' and *les* is translated as 'them'. The preceding direct object must agree with the noun it refers to in terms of gender and number.

DON'T FORGET

Ne ... jamais is a negative phrase. Refer to pages 8–9 to revise negatives. Negatives usually sandwich the verb. When using a negative phrase with a preceding direct object, the negatives sandwich both the preceding direct object and the verb, for example *je **ne** le regarde **jamais*** – I never watch it.

VIDEO LINK

Check out the clip 'My favourite films and directors' at www.brightredbooks.net/N5French

ACTIVITY: PRECEDING DIRECT OBJECTS

Now try to translate the following sentences using the correct preceding direct object.

1. I like westerns. I watch them often.

2. I love comedies. I watch them at weekends.

3. I don't like documentaries. I watch them rarely.

4. I hate football. I watch it sometimes.

5. I like the weather. I watch it every day.

6. I don't like crime films. I never watch them.

ONLINE TEST

Try the 'Watching TV – Regarder la télé' test online at www.brightredbooks.net/N5French

THINGS TO DO AND THINK ABOUT

Now write a paragraph about how much time you spend watching TV, what you watch on TV and why. Refer back to the section on opinion phrases on page 25 and try to include them. You may wish to use this as part of your Performance if you talk about what you do during your free time.

REALITY TV – LA TÉLÉ-RÉALITÉ

Reality TV shows have become very popular amongst young people. What do you think are the advantages and disadvantages of reality TV?

DON'T FORGET

Try to pick out phrases you could use in your performance about the advantages and disadvantages of watching reality TV when reading the text on page 37.

 **ACTIVITY** FOR OR AGAINST REALITY TV – POUR OU CONTRE LA TÉLÉ-RÉALITÉ

Read the conversation between Mathieu and Lucie and answer the questions below. Here are some tips for how to approach a reading comprehension as part of the Unit and Course assessments.

- Start by reading the background information as this will tell you what the text is about.

- Read the questions carefully.

- The answers usually come in the same order as the questions, so the questions might also give you an idea of what the text is about.

- Pick out key words from the questions and use these to predict key words that you might see in the text.

- Look at the number of marks given for each question so you know how much information to give in your answers.

- When you read a word that you don't understand, try to make links with English words, refer to the glossary or use your dictionary to look up what they mean.

contd

Mathieu and Lucie

M: Salut Lucie, est-ce que tu as vu l'émission qui s'appelle 'Secret Story' hier soir? C'était génial. Ça m'a fait beaucoup rire et je l'ai trouvé vraiment divertissante.

L: Non, j'ai horreur des émissions de télé-réalité. La télé-réalité est devenue plus populaire depuis quelques années. Elle n'apporte rien d'utile pour la société. En plus, il est difficile d'échapper aux émissions de télé-réalité car il y en a trop.

M: Je ne suis pas d'accord. Les téléspectateurs la trouvent captivante. En effet mes parents disent que je suis accro. Selon moi, il s'agit d'un concours où les gens ont envie de gagner beaucoup d'argent ou de devenir célèbres. On voudrait réaliser son rêve, comme devenir chanteur célèbre et de temps en temps il y a des gens avec beaucoup de talent. Souvent ce sont les gens ordinaires qui participent aux emissions de télé-réalité. Je vote toujours pour les participants que je préfère.

L: Est-ce que tu plaisantes? Est-ce que tu ne te rends pas compte que c'est totalement faux, ce n'est pas la réalité. Ce que je n'aime pas, c'est que parfois les candidats font des choses choquantes et gênantes. Je pense que la télé-réalité a une mauvaise influence sur les jeunes. Les jeunes croient qu'on ne doit pas travailler dur au lycée car ils peuvent devenir riches rapidement grâce aux émissions de télé-réalité. Ça leur donne l'impression qu'il suffit de participer à une émission de télé-réalité pour être célèbre et pour être riche. Il y a des gens qui contribuent à la société en faisant beaucoup de choses pour aider les autres et à mon avis ce sont eux qui devraient recevoir de l'argent et de la publicité, pas les participants d'une emission bête.

M: Pour moi, le plus intéressant c'est observer la vie de gens et leur relations avec les autres. A mon avis on peut mieux comprendre la nature humaine en regardant ce genre d'émission. Ce que j'aime le plus, c'est que ces émissions me donnent l'espoir que ma vie peut changer facilement aussi. Peut-être que je vais m'inscrire à la prochaine série de 'Secret Story'.

Questions

1. Why did Mathieu enjoy watching the programme 'Secret Story'? (2)

2. How does Lucie describe reality TV? (2)

3. Why does she think it is difficult to escape reality TV programmes? (1)

4. What does Mathieu say the programmes are about? (1)

5. What does Mathieu always do? (1)

6. What does Lucie not like and why? (1)

7. What does Lucie say about reality TV and young people? (1)

8. According to Lucie, what do young people believe? (2)

9. Who does Lucie say deserves publicity and money? (1)

10. What does Mathieu find interesting about these programmes? (2)

ONLINE

Check out the BrightRED Digital Zone for the answers to all the activities in this section: www.brightredbooks.net/N5French

DON'T FORGET

When giving your opinion on something, always try to give a reason, introducing it with *car*, *parce que* or *pour* + infinitive.

DON'T FORGET

Make use of the Glossary at the back of the book if you need to check the meaning of any of the words here.

ONLINE TEST

Take the 'Reality TV – La télé-réalité' test online at www.brightredbooks.net/N5French

THINGS TO DO AND THINK ABOUT

Using the text, pick out some phrases that reflect how you feel about reality TV.
Write a paragraph on reality TV. Don't forget to use **opinion phrases** and **conjunctions**.
You may wish to use this paragraph in your Performance.

TECHNOLOGY – LA TECHNOLOGIE

Technology has a huge part to play in our daily lives, from using your mobile phone to using the internet to shop for clothes. How many different forms of technology do you use regularly? Here are a few to help you get started:

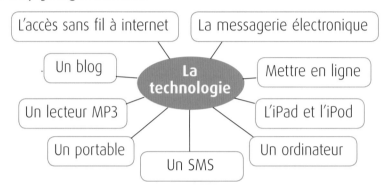

L'accès sans fil à internet

La messagerie électronique

Un blog

La technologie

Mettre en ligne

Un lecteur MP3

L'iPad et l'iPod

Un portable

Un ordinateur

Un SMS

ACTIVITY USE OF TECHNOLOGY – L'USAGE DE LA TECHNOLOGIE

It would be useful to be able to say how you use technology. Read the following phrases, put them into the first person (the *je* form) and translate them into English. The first one has been put into first person for you.

Listen to the phrases online to help you with the pronunciation.

- Envoyer des SMS/des textos à ses amis avec son portable – J'envoie des SMS/des textos à mes amis avec mon portable
- Réserver des places de concerts en ligne
- Pouvoir télécharger des films et de la musique
- Faire de la recherche pour ses devoirs
- Prendre des photos avec son portable
- Commander des livres en ligne
- Surfer le net pour trouver les renseignements
- Envoyer des émails
- Utiliser Internet pour écouter de la musique ou regarder des films
- Tchater dans les forums pour rencontrer des amis
- Faire du shopping en ligne
- Rester en contact avec ses cousins à l'étranger grâce au net
- Retirer de l'argent au distributeur automatique
- Acheter les billets d'avion et réserver un hôtel pour les vacances sur le net
- Jouer à des jeux en ligne

DON'T FORGET

Use a dictionary to check any verbs that you are unfamiliar with.

ONLINE

Head to www. brightredbooks.net/subjects/ n5french/c02_18 for an extra activity on the internet.

 **ACTIVITY:** ADVANTAGES AND DISADVANTAGES OF TECHNOLOGY – LES AVANTAGES ET LES INCONVÉNIENTS DE LA TECHNOLOGIE

There are many advantages and disadvantages of using technology.

First, read the following phrases and try to work out what they mean before listening to them. Use a dictionary to look up any unfamiliar vocabulary.

Then listen to the phrases online and put them under the correct heading of either *Avantages* or *Inconvénients*.

Finally, note down the reason(s) why they are advantages or disadvantages.

Transcript

1. La vie de tous les jours est plus facile grâce à la technologie. Je ne sais pas ce que je ferais sans mon portable. Je peux rester en contact avec mes amis et mes parents de n'importe où.

2. Selon moi, avoir un portable coûte très cher et c'est une perte d'argent. En plus l'utilisation du téléphone portable peut être dangereuse pour la santé. Les portables, ce n'est pas mon truc.

3. J'adore le monde virtuel. Je suis un vrai internaute car je fais tout sur le net. J'achète mes vêtements, je télécharge la musique et les films en ligne, ce qui est moins cher qu'acheter les CDs et les DVDs.

4. Pour moi, la technologie, c'est formidable. Mon site préféré, c'est le Facebook car je peux communiquer avec mes amis. C'est très rapide et on peut y voir les photos de ses amis immédiatement. On peut aussi exprimer ses idées et ses opinions.

5. Je pense que les sites communautaires peuvent être dangereux car on peut rencontrer des gens bizarres quand on tchate en ligne. Il y a des gens menaçants qui se cachent derrière leurs écrans.

6. Je passe des heures à trouver les produits en ligne car il y a plus de choix sur le net que dans les magasins. En plus je peux comparer les prix et acheter les produits les moins chers.

7. Je suis technophobe. Je déteste les ordinateurs car ils sont compliqués. Je ne comprends pas le langage de technologie.

8. Il existe des dangers sur le net. Les parents s'inquiètent pour la sécurité de leurs enfants car les jeunes peuvent être victimes d'intimidation sur le net.

9. On dépend trop de son téléphone portable et en effet, certains disent qu'ils ne pourraient pas survivre sans leur portable. On envoie des SMS et des messages électroniques, on parle aux amis, on lit des livres, on surfe sur le net, on joue à des jeux et on écoute de la musique. On passe trop de temps sur son portable et par conséquent, il y a moins de communication entre les personnes.

10. Ce que j'aime le plus, c'est que je peux écouter de la musique sur mon iPod sans déranger personne. Je peux aussi lire des livres en tout genre sur le même écran avec mon Kindle, ce qui est génial.

Try out Activity 1 in the end of chapter activities on the BrightRED Digital Zone for a great translation exercise about using the internet.

 ## THINGS TO DO AND THINK ABOUT

Choose five phrases to describe how you use technology. Try to include three advantages and three disadvantages of using technology. You may wish to learn them for your Performance and you could also use them as part of your writing about leisure and hobbies.

 ONLINE TEST

Why not try the 'Technology – La technologie' test at www.brightredbooks.net/N5French?

YOUR HOME AREA AS A TOURIST AREA – TA REGION COMME LIEU TOURISTIQUE

In this section, you will learn to describe why tourists might come to your home area. We will revise how to say where you live and then learn to say what is in your town that tourists might want to come and see.

WHERE DO YOU LIVE? – OÙ HABITES-TU?

Let's start off by saying where in Scotland you live:

J'habite à ... en Écosse.

Grammar

To say that you live in a town and in a country, you need to know the following:

J'habite à + name of place (Glasgow/Paris)
J'habite *en* + feminine country: en Écosse
J'habite *au* + masculine country: au Pays de Galles
J'habite *aux* + plural country: aux États-Unis

⚙ ACTIVITY: WHERE YOU LIVE – LÀ, OÙ TU HABITES

(a) Now try and fill in the blanks with the correct word: *à, en, au, aux*. Use your dictionary to find out the gender of the country.

1. J'habite ___ Edimbourg.
2. J'habite ___ Pays-Bas.
3. J'habite ___ Espagne.
4. J'habite ___ Inverness.
5. J'habite ___ Portugal.
6. J'habite ___ Italie.

(b) Let's look at the points of the compass to say where in Scotland you live. Can you complete the points of the compass?

(c) Do you live in a city or a town or in the countryside? Match the French to the English and use a dictionary to look up any unfamiliar vocabulary.

1. à la campagne	A. in the countryside
2. à la montagne	B. in town
3. au bord de la mer	C. in the outskirts/suburbs
4. dans une grande ville	D. in the mountains
5. dans un village	E. in the town centre
6. en ville	F. at the seaside
7. au centre-ville	G. in a city
8. en banlieue	H. in a village

DON'T FORGET ➕

Try to make links between the French and English vocabulary to work out what the words mean.

(d) Now complete the sentences about where you live:

- J'habite à ... (name of place)
- Ma ville/mon village se trouve dans le/l'... de l'Ecosse. (location)
- J'habite ... (town/countryside etc.)

ACTIVITY: DESCRIBING YOUR AREA – DÉCRIRE TON QUARTIER

It would be useful to be able to describe the area in which you live. Can you think of any adjectives that you could use to describe your home area? Here are a few to start off. Look up any words you are not familiar with in the dictionary. Then put the adjectives under the headings: positif/négatif.

- agréable
- amusant(e)
- animé(e)
- beau/belle
- ancien(ne)
- historique
- industriel(le)
- joli(e)
- magnifique
- moderne
- pittoresque
- pollué(e)
- propre
- touristique
- tranquille

ACTIVITY: MY HOME TOWN – MA VILLE

Listen to the following texts online and fill in the blanks using the words in the box below. Read the text first to get the gist of what it is about and try to predict what you are going to hear.

A. J'habite à Aberdeen. C'est une _____ _____qui se trouve dans le _____ de l'Écosse. Je pense que c'est une ville _____, dynamique et _____.

B. J'habite à West Linton. C'est un _____ _____ qui est situé près d'Édimbourg dans le _____ de l'Écosse. Je trouve que, c'est un village historique, _____ et pittoresque.

C. J'habite à Girvan. C'est une ville moyenne qui se trouve __ ___ __ __ ___dans le _____ de l'Écosse. Je pense que c'est une ville ____, jolie et _____.

> au bord de la mer   petit village   touristique   industriel   propre
> grande ville   animé   nord-est   centre   sud-ouest   tranquille

 ONLINE TEST

Take the 'Your home area as a tourist area – Ton quartier comme lieu touristique' test online at www.brightredbooks.net/N5French

THINGS TO DO AND THINK ABOUT

Can you write a short paragraph to describe exactly where you live and what it is like? Use the language in this section to help you. You may wish to use this as part of your writing and Performance.

A TOURIST TOWN – UNE VILLE TOURISTIQUE

Can you think of what tourists visiting your home area might like to do? Think about the following:

Qu'est-ce qu'on peut faire dans ta ville? What can you do in your town?

ACTIVITY: MY TOWN – MA VILLE

Read the following texts and answer the questions. You should look for key words and verbs that will help you to identify why their home area is a good place for tourists to visit. Try to give as much information as possible in your answers.

Philippe

J'habite dans une petite ville pittoresque. En été, il y a plein de touristes qui visitent notre ville car elle se trouve au bord de la mer. On peut se promener à la plage et se balader dans la ville pour voir de beaux bâtiments. C'est un endroit idéal pour les jeunes actifs qui adorent faire des sports aquatiques. On peut faire de la planche à voile et de la plongée. En plus, on peut louer des bateaux, ce qui est vraiment amusant. Il y a des auberges de jeunesse où on peut loger pendant son séjour. En plus, il y a quelques petits restaurants typiques qui sont très populaires car la nourriture y est délicieuse.

1. Where does Philippe live? (2)

2. Name any three things that tourists can do when they visit his town in summer. (3)

3. Where can they stay in the town? (1)

4. What does he say is popular and why? (2)

Sandrine

J'habite dans une grande ville animée qui est célèbre parmi les touristes car il y a beaucoup de choses à faire et à voir. Tout d'abord, on peut visiter un grand château ancien et il y a aussi beaucoup de monuments historiques. Si on aime l'histoire ou les œuvres d'art, il y a un grand choix de musées et de galeries où on peut y passer des heures. Le soir, on peut voir des spectacles au théâtre ou on peut aller aux concerts. L'activité la plus populaire pour les touristes, c'est découvrir des monuments à bord d'un bus touristique qui fait le tour de la ville. Pour les enfants, il y a un bowling, une patinoire et un grand parc public. En plus, il y a beaucoup d'hôtels de quatre et cinq étoiles et des appartements de luxe qu'on peut louer.

1. Where does Sandrine live? (1)

2. Why is it famous amongst tourists? (1)

contd

3. Name three places that you can visit there. (3)

4. What can you do in the evening? (2)

5. What is the most popular activity amongst tourists? (1)

6. What three places does Sandrine say would be good for children? (3)

7. Where can tourists stay? (2)

Jean-Luc

Mon village se trouve à la montagne. C'est assez petit mais c'est bien connu parmi les touristes à cause des montagnes. Si on aime faire de la randonnée, mon village est l'endroit idéal. En hiver, quand il neige, on peut faire du ski. J'ai de la chance d'y habiter car le ski, c'est mon sport préféré. On peut loger dans un petit hôtel de trois étoiles, qui est situé dans la rue principale. On peut manger dans les pubs et il y a aussi un restaurant traditionnel. Malheureusement, ce que je n'aime pas c'est qu'il n'y a pas beaucoup de choses à faire le soir car il n'y a pas de cinéma ou de théâtre. Pourtant en été il y a des gens qui viennent d'autres pays pour aller aux festivals et aux fêtes de musique traditionnelle qui ont lieu près de mon village, ce qui est génial.

1. Where does Jean-Luc live? (2)

2. What can you do in the area? (2)

3. Where can you stay? (1)

4. Where can you eat? (2)

5. What does he not like about where he lives? (1)

6. What happens in the summer? (2)

Marie-Claire

J'habite en banlieue d'une grande ville dynamique et multiculturelle. Ce que j'aime le plus, c'est qu'il y a plein de touristes qui visitent ma ville pendant toute l'année et il y a une atmosphère animée. Les touristes aiment faire les magasins, acheter des souvenirs et manger dans de bons restaurants traditionnels. On peut aussi faire du tourisme car il y a également plein de sites touristiques. Si on veut voir un peu de la région, on peut visiter les lacs, les montagnes et les distilleries écossaises. En plus, on peut se déplacer facilement car il y a un bon système de transport en commun. Finalement, il y a un bon choix d'hébergement, comme les hôtels, les auberges de jeunesse et les pensions où on peut loger.

1. Where does Marie-Claire live? (3)

2. What does she like the most about her town? (2)

3. Name any three things tourists can do in Marie Claire's city. (3)

4. What can you visit in the region? (3)

5. What does she say about transport? (2)

6. Where can you stay? (3)

DON'T FORGET

For more activities, look at the section on sports and hobbies on page 23.

DON'T FORGET

Il y a un musée means 'there is a museum' and *il n'y a pas de cinéma* means 'there isn't a cinema'. *Il n'y a pas* is followed by *de*.

ONLINE TEST

Take the 'A tourist town – Une ville touristique' test online at www. brightredbooks.net/N5French

THINGS TO DO AND THINK ABOUT

Using the language in this unit, write a paragraph about what there is for tourists to do in your home area. Think about it in terms of location, activities, accommodation and eating out. You can learn this and you may wish to use it as part of your Performance.

TOWN AND COUNTRY – LA VILLE ET LA CAMPAGNE 1

In this section, we will compare life in a town or city to life in the countryside. Can you think of any obvious differences between the different ways of life?

DON'T FORGET

The language used to describe life in the countryside could be adapted to describe life at the seaside if you live by the sea, for example *C'est tranquille au bord de la mer*.

ONLINE

Visit the 'Answers' section at www.brightredbooks.net/N5French to check how you got on!

DON'T FORGET

Beaucoup and *trop* are useful words and they are often followed by *de*: *beaucoup de choses* means 'a lot of things' and *trop de choses* means 'too many things'. Other examples of words that follow this pattern include *plein de* and *assez de*.

DON'T FORGET

Près de and *loin de* are called **prepositions** and they tell us the position of something. Can you think of any other prepositions?

 **ACTIVITY** DESCRIPTION OF THE TOWN AND THE COUNTRYSIDE – LA DESCRIPTION DE LA VILLE ET DE LA CAMPAGNE

Have a look at the following adjectives. Do you recognise any of them? If there are any unfamiliar words, look up their meaning in the dictionary and then decide if the words best describe life in the town or in the countryside. Could they be used to describe both areas?

- Tranquille
- Cosmopolite
- Calme
- Beau/belle
- Pollué(e)
- Reposant(e)
- Stressant(e)
- Animé(e)
- Ennuyeux/ennuyeuse
- Divertissant(e)
- Vert(e)
- Bruyant(e)
- Isolé(e)
- Cher/chère
- Sale

ACTIVITY THE TOWN – LA VILLE

We will now focus on life in a town or a city.

Read the following phrases and try to work out what the words mean by identifying familiar vocabulary. Try to work out the meaning of unfamiliar French vocabulary by making links to English words. Translate the phrases into English using a bilingual dictionary. List the phrases as either advantages or disadvantages of living in a town/city.

1. C'est bruyant.
2. Il y a beaucoup de pollution.
3. Il y a beaucoup de choses à faire et à voir.
4. On peut faire du tourisme en visitant les monuments historiques et les sites touristiques.
5. Il y a beaucoup de déchets par terre.
6. Il y a un bon choix de restaurants.
7. Il y a trop de circulation.
8. On peut faire les magasins au centre-ville.
9. La vie nocturne est géniale.
10. On peut sortir en boîte de nuit.
11. Il y a beaucoup de moyens de faire du sport.
12. Il y a trop de monde.
13. Les loyers sont chers.
14. On peut se déplacer facilement grâce aux transports en commun.
15. Il n'y a pas assez d'espaces verts.
16. Il y a plein de divertissements pour les jeunes.
17. La vie peut être stressante.
18. On peut profiter de la vie culturelle comme le théâtre et les musées.
19. On ne connaît pas ses voisins.
20. On ne se sent pas en sécurité.

ACTIVITY THE COUNTRYSIDE – LA CAMPAGNE

We will now do the same exercise for the countryside.

Read the French phrases and try to work out what they mean by making links to English or using a bilingual dictionary. Translate the phrases into English (good practice for Higher French!). List the phrases as either advantages or disadvantages of living in the countryside.

contd

1. On est isolé.
2. Il n'y a rien à faire pour les jeunes.
3. Le paysage est vraiment beau.
4. Il faut avoir une voiture pour se déplacer.
5. Le mode de vie est reposant.
6. Tout le monde se connaît.
7. La vie peut être ennuyeuse et monotone.
8. Il faut aller en ville pour étudier car il n'y a pas de lycées ou d'universités.
9. On n'est pas pressé.
10. Il n'y a pas de distractions.
11. Il y a plein d'espaces verts.
12. C'est assez propre.
13. C'est tranquille et paisible.
14. Il n'y a pas de commodités à proximité.
15. L'air est pur car il y a moins de pollution.
16. On peut faire de longues promenades.
17. On peut se détendre.
18. On vit près de la nature.
19. Il y a peu de possibilités de trouver un bon emploi.
20. Il y a moins de violence.
21. On habite loin de ses amis.
22. Tout le monde s'intéresse trop à la vie des autres.
23. Il y a moins de bruit.
24. Les transports en commun ne sont pas efficaces.

GRAMMAR: COMPARATIVES AND SUPERLATIVES

In this section, you have been comparing the town to the countryside. You will have noticed phrases like:

- il y a *moins* de pollution
- la vie à la campagne est *plus* reposante *que* la vie en ville
- ce que j'aime *le plus* ...

In English we can compare things by putting 'er' at the end of an adjective (smaller, taller) or by saying something is 'the _____est' (e.g. the smallest, the tallest). In French we use the following to compare things:

- plus ... (que)   more ... (than)
- moins ... (que)   less ... (than)
- aussi ... (que)   just as ... (as)
- le/la/les plus ...   the most ...
- le/la/les moins ...   the least ...

For example:

- John est petit   John is small.
- Peter est plus petit (que John).   Peter is smaller (than John).
- Peter est aussi petit que Jacques.   Peter is as small as Jacques.
- Jack est *le* plus petit.   Jack is the smallest.
- Marie est *la* plus peti**t**e.   Marie is the smallest.

Be careful, as there are some exceptions:

Adjective	Comparative	Superlative
bon(ne)(s)(nes) (good)	meilleur(e)(s)(es) (better)	le/la/les meilleur(e)(s)(es) (the best)
mauvais(e)(es) (bad)	pire(s) (worse)	le/la/les pire(s) (the worst)

For example:

- Le café est meilleur que le thé.   Coffee is better than tea.
- Le chocolat chaud est le meilleur.   Hot chocolate is the best.

ONLINE TEST

Take the 'Prepositions' test at www.brightredbooks.net/N5French

THINGS TO DO AND THINK ABOUT

Now try to write a short paragraph about the advantages and disadvantages of living in the town and the countryside. How many of the phrases from the above sections can you remember? You may wish to use this as part of your Performance.

TOWN AND COUNTRY – LA VILLE ET LA CAMPAGNE 2

 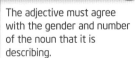
 **ACTIVITY** COMPARATIVE AND SUPERLATIVE

Now try to translate the following sentences using the **comparative** and **superlative**.

1. The town is more fun than the countryside.
2. The town is less boring than the countryside.
3. The town is the most fun.
4. The countryside is the most boring.
5. The town is the least boring.
6. The countryside is the least fun.
7. The town is the best.
8. The countryside is the worst.

 **ACTIVITY** TOWN OR COUNTRYSIDE – LA VILLE OU LA CAMPAGNE

Read the following two texts and answer the following questions:

1. Where did each person used to live?
2. What did they like about it?
3. Where do they live now?
4. What do they like about it?
5. Where would they prefer to live if they had the choice and why?

Corine

Quand j'étais petite, j'habitais à la campagne. On a déménagé car mon père a trouvé un nouveau boulot. J'aimais la vie à la campagne car on connaissait tout le monde et on avait beaucoup de liberté. On pouvait jouer dehors quand il faisait beau car il y avait plein d'espaces verts. Maintenant, nous habitons dans une grande ville. Ce que j'aime le plus, c'est que tous mes amis habitent près de chez moi. Il est facile de se déplacer et il y a toujours quelque chose à faire comme aller au cinéma ou faire les magasins au centre commercial. Si j'avais le choix, j'habiterais en ville parce que la ville est plus animée que la campagne. En plus, il y a énormément de distractions pour les jeunes.

Bernard

Quand j'étais plus jeune, j'habitais en ville. J'aimais la vie en ville car on pouvait se déplacer facilement et il y avait beaucoup de distractions. Par contre, il y avait trop de monde, trop de pollution et trop de bruit en ville. Maintenant, nous habitons à la campagne. J'adore la vie à la campagne car il y a moins de crime et de violence donc on se sent en sécurité. En plus, j'aime vivre près de la nature et passer mon temps libre à faire des randonnées à pied. Si j'avais le choix, j'habiterais à la campagne car j'adore la tranquillité et le mode de vie paisible.

Now look at this third text about life at the seaside.

Delphine

Avant j'habitais dans une ville moyenne au bord de la mer. La vie était vraiment passionnante car il y avait toujours beaucoup de choses à faire. Normalement, on aimait passer le week-end à la plage. On faisait de longues promenades, on faisait des sports nautiques, comme la planche à voile ou on jouait au volley. C'était génial. On est parti de la ville quand j'avais onze ans. La vie est vraiment calme à la campagne et au début, je l'ai trouvé ennuyeuse. Je me suis habituée à la tranquillité et je dirais que maintenant, je préfère vivre à la campagne. Ce que j'aime le plus, c'est qu'il n'y a pas de touristes en été et il y a moins de circulation. À l'avenir, si j'ai le choix, j'habiterai en ville car je voudrais aller à l'université pour étudier les langues étrangères.

contd

KNOWLEDGE ABOUT LANGUAGE

What do you notice about the verbs in the three reading texts? Can you spot the different tenses that we have already learned?

Can you spot the verbs in the present tense? Refer to page 7 to revise the present tense.

Can you pick out verbs in the perfect tense? Refer to pages 67–9 to revise the perfect tense.

Can you pick out verbs in the imperfect tense? Refer to page 45 to revise the imperfect tense.

What about the future and conditional tenses? Refer to page 88 to revise the future and conditional tenses.

DON'T FORGET

Look for time phrases to help you identify the different tenses, for example *maintenant* indicates an action happening in the present tense while *à l'avenir* refers to actions happening in the future.

GRAMMAR: THE IMPERFECT TENSE – L'IMPARFAIT

Take another look at the sections which describe where each person used to live and see if you can work out a pattern. The tense used is called the imperfect tense or l'imparfait.

We use the imperfect tense:
- to describe a past repeated action
- to describe what something or someone *was* like in the past
- to say what someone *used to do*
- to describe an interrupted action in the past – to say what someone/something was doing when something else happened.

How do we form the imperfect tense?
1. Start with the 'nous' form of the verb in the present tense.
2. Take off the '-ons' to form the stem.
3. Add the imperfect ending.

e.g. Jouer– to play.
1. Start with the 'nous' part in the present tense: *nous jouons.*
2. Take off '-ons': *jou.*
3. Add endings:

je jou*ais*	I used to play/was playing
tu jou*ais*	you used to play/were playing
il jou*ait*	he used to play/was playing
elle jou*ait*	she used to play/was playing
on jou*ait*	we used to play/were playing

nous jou*ions*	we used to play/were playing
vous jou*iez*	you used to play/were playing
ils jou*aient*	they used to play/were playing
elles jou*aient*	they used to play/were playing

You will be pleased to know that there is only one irregular verb in the imperfect tense, être – it uses the same endings, but the stem is 'ét':

j'étais	I was/used to be
tu étais	you were/used to be
il etait	he was/used to be
elle était	she was/used to be
on était	we were/used to be

nous étions	we were/used to be
vous étiez	you were/used to be
ils étaient	they were/used to be
elles étaient	they were/used to be

Try the end of chapter activities on the Digital Zone for extra practice on the imperfect tense.

THINGS TO DO AND THINK ABOUT

- Make up a paragraph about where you used to live and what you liked or didn't like (it doesn't have to be true!).
- Then describe where you live now give your opinions about what you think of it and reasons for your opinions.
- To finish, say where you would like to live.

This is your chance to show how good you are so try to use different tenses, time phrases, linking words, comparatives, superlatives and opinion phrases. You may wish to use this as part of your Performance.

ENVIRONMENT – L'ENVIRONNEMENT

Can you think of different ways that you can be environmentally friendly at home? Here are a few to help you get started:

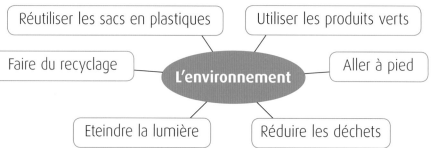

Réutiliser les sacs en plastiques

Utiliser les produits verts

Faire du recyclage

L'environnement

Aller à pied

Eteindre la lumière

Réduire les déchets

⚙ ACTIVITY: PROBLEMS WITH OUR ENVIRONMENT – LES PROBLÈMES DE L'ENVIRONNEMENT

Let's start off by looking at the environmental problems that we are faced with. Read the phrases and translate them into English. Can you work out what they mean by making links to English phrases to do with environmental problems? If there are any phrases you are unsure of, use a bilingual dictionary to look them up.

1. La déforestation
2. Le réchauffement de la terre et le changement climatique
3. La pollution de l'air à cause des véhicules
4. La circulation et les embouteillages
5. La sécheresse
6. L'extinction des espèces menacées
7. L'effet de serre et le trou dans la couche d'ozone
8. La pluie acide à cause des activités industrielles
9. Les déchets
10. L'emballage
11. Le gaspillage d'énergie
12. La pollution de l'eau

⚙ ACTIVITY PROTECTING THE ENVIRONMENT – PROTÉGER L'ENVIRONNEMENT

Read through the following ways to help to protect our environment and translate them into English. Then match them to the problems above.

1. Il faut utiliser l'essence sans plomb.
2. Il faut protéger les espèces menacées, par exemple les animaux qui habitent dans les forêts tropicales.
3. Il faut aller à pied ou utiliser les transports en commun.
4. Il faut planter des arbres.
5. Il faut limiter l'utilisation des CFC.
6. On doit trier les déchets pour recycler le papier, le plastique et le verre.
7. Il faut réduire la consommation d'eau en fermant le robinet et en prenant une douche au lieu d'un bain.
8. Il faut utiliser les énergies renouvelables et réduire la production de gaz carbonique.
9. Il faut réduire les déchets et éviter le gaspillage.
10. Il faut éviter de jeter les ordures dans la mer.
11. Il faut réduire les émissions des usines et la consommation de combustibles fossiles.
12. Il faut conserver l'énergie et utiliser plus d'énergies propres et renouvelables, comme l'énergie solaire, l'énergie éolienne ou hydroulique.

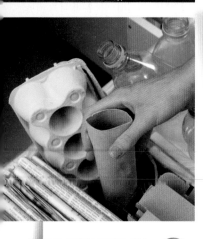

DON'T FORGET ➕

Il faut is a useful phrase meaning 'we must' or 'it is necessary to' and it is always followed by the infinitive.

ACTIVITY: MODAL VERBS – LES VERBES MODAUX

Have a go at Activity 4 in the end of chapter activities (on the BrightRED Digital Zone), which will help you with the next exercise.

Following the listening activity, try to complete this task.

1. Look at the infinitives in the box below and work out what they mean.

2. Complete the sentences.

3. Try to translate the sentences – this will be good practice for Higher French!

Only look at the text from the listening if you get stuck, otherwise use your common sense to fill in the blanks with the appropriate verb.

1. Il faut _____ les matériaux recyclables, comme les journaux, le verre et le plastique.

2. On doit _____ du papier recyclé et des piles rechargeables au supermarché.

3. On devrait _____ les sacs en plastique.

4. On pourrait _____ la consommation d'eau.

5. On peut _____ les produits écologiques à la maison.

6. On devrait _____ à pied ou en transport en commun.

7. Il faut _____ les lumières quand on quitte une pièce.

8. On ne devrait pas _____ l'énergie.

9. On doit _____ l'environnement.

10. Au lieu de _____ un bain, il faut se doucher.

| acheter | prendre | réduire | éteindre | gaspiller | recycler | aller | protéger |
| réutiliser | utiliser |

ONLINE

Before you complete this activity, try out Activity 4 in the end of chapter activities at www.brightredbooks.net/N5French

DON'T FORGET

On doit and *on devrait* come from the verb *devoir*, meaning 'to have to' or 'must', and *on peut* and *on pourrait* come from the verb *pouvoir*, meaning 'to be able to' or 'can'. Modal verbs are always followed by the infinitive.

VIDEO LINK

Watch the clips 'Le recyclage au Canada' and 'Protéger l'eau' at www.brightredbooks.net/N5French

ONLINE TEST

Take the 'Environment – L'environnement' test online at www.brightredbooks.net/N5French

THINGS TO DO AND THINK ABOUT

Write a short essay about what you and your family do to help the environment. Try to use some of the opening sentences and conjunctions from Activity 4 in the end of chapter activities (www.brightredbooks.net/N5French). This could be used as part of your Performance. You could structure it in the following way:

Introduction: What is your short essay about? Name a few environmental problems.

Je voudrais écrire au sujet de l'environnement. De nos jours il y a des problèmes de l'environnement comme ...

Paragraph 1: What environmental problems are there?

C'est vrai qu'il y a beaucoup de problèmes d'environnement. Par exemple, ...

Paragraph 2: What should everyone do?

Il faut/Il ne faut pas/On doit/On ne doit pas/On devrait/On ne devrait pas/On peut + infinitive

Paragraph 3: What you do:

Je .../Ma famille .../Mes parents ... (see the phrases used in the listening transcript from Activity 4 in the end of chapter activities on the Digital Zone)

Conclusion:

En somme, il est important de protéger notre planète.

LEARNING

SCHOOL SUBJECTS – LES MATIÈRES

In this chapter we will look at the context of learning. The topics we will cover include:

- Learning activities you enjoy
- Learning activities you don't enjoy
- Preparing for exams
- Comparing education systems in Scotland to other systems
- How to improve education systems

ONLINE TEST

Take the test 'School subjects – Les matières' at www.brightredbooks.net/N5French.

REVISION – LA REVISION

At this stage, it would be worth revising school subjects. How many can you remember off the top of your head?

 ACTIVITY LEARNING ACTIVITIES – LES ACTIVITÉS D'APPRENTISSAGE

Think about the range of activities you do in each subject. Can you work out what the following activities mean in English?

1. Apprendre le vocabulaire
2. Résoudre les problèmes
3. Travailler tout(e) seul(e)
4. Travailler en groupe/en équipe
5. Travailler à deux
6. Travailler à l'ordinateur
7. Copier les notes du tableau
8. Regarder les documentaires
9. Lire
10. Chercher les mots dans le dictionnaire
11. Faire des recherches
12. Rédiger des dissertations
13. Créer
14. Dessiner
15. Faire les devoirs
16. Faire des présentations
17. Jouer des instruments
18. Faire des activités sportives
19. Participer aux jeux
20. Écouter le prof

contd

21. Communiquer avec ses camarades de classe

22. Faire de l'arithmétique et de l'algèbre

23. Faire des travaux manuels comme le bricolage

24. Cuisiner

25. Apprendre la grammaire

26. Apprendre l'orthographe

27. Passer les examens (oraux/écrits)

28. Faire des expériences scientifiques

 **ACTIVITY:** SUBJECTS AND ACTIVITIES – LES MATIÈRES ET LES ACTIVITÉS

1. Write a list in French of the subjects you are currently studying at school.

2. Beside each subject write at least one activity that you do in this subject. Try to put the infinitives into the 'je' form (refer to page 7 if you need to revise how to form the present tense). Look up the verb section in your dictionary to check any irregular verbs.

 **ACTIVITY:** WHAT DO YOU LIKE DOING AT SCHOOL/ COLLEGE OR UNIVERSITY? – QU'EST-CE QUE TU AIMES FAIRE AU LYCÉE/À LA FAC?

 DON'T FORGET

When giving your opinion in French remember that phrases like *j'aime, j'adore, je n'aime pas, je déteste* and *je préfère* are all followed by the verb in the infinitive, for example *j'aime travailler* means 'I like to work', but often in English we translate it as 'I like working'.

Now that you have decided which activities you do in different subjects, you will learn how to give your opinion of the different activities. Refer to page 25 to revise opinion phrases before you start this exercise.

Listen to the following four people discussing what they like and dislike doing at school and complete the table below. Write as much as you can under each heading (you may need to use extra paper).

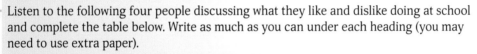

Name	Subject	Activities they enjoy	Reason	Activities they dislike	Reason
Frédéric					
Corinne					
Thierry					
Anna					

 THINGS TO DO AND THINK ABOUT

Can you write about some of the learning activities you do at school? Try to include:

● which activities you do in different subjects

● which activities you enjoy

● which activities you do not enjoy.

Don't forget to give reasons for your opinions. You may wish to use this as part of your Performance.

 VIDEO LINK

Check out the clip 'Les cours et les devoirs' at www. brightredbooks.net/N5French

PREPARING FOR EXAMS 1 – SE PREPARER AUX EXAMENS

As you are using this book, it is likely you are preparing for your French exams. In this section we will look at different types of exams and how best to prepare for them.

DON'T FORGET

Passer mes examens is a false friend meaning 'to sit an exam', not 'to pass an exam' and *assister à* means 'to attend', not 'to assist'.

ACTIVITY: SITTING EXAMS – PASSER LES EXAMENS

Let's start by thinking about how you might introduce talking about your exams. We all strive to do well and, by getting good grades in your exams, you will have a lot of opportunities open to you. We will start by saying what exams you are sitting and that you need to work hard this year to succeed. Can you work out what the following phrases mean?

1. Cette année je passe mes examens de National 5.

2. J'étudie six matières, y compris les maths, l'anglais, le français, l'histoire, la musique et la biologie.

3. Je suis en train de me préparer aux examens de National 5.

4. Je vais passer mes examens de National 5 à la fin de l'année scolaire.

5. Je voudrais réussir à mes examens cette année car j'ai l'intention de continuer mes études l'année prochaine.

6. Si j'ai de bonnes notes, je pourrai trouver un bon emploi à l'avenir.

7. Je dois beaucoup travailler pour réussir à mes examens.

8. Je dois travailler dur(e) pour réussir à mes examens car j'ai envie de quitter le lycée et trouver un bon emploi.

At this point, you could link why you want to do well in your exams to your future plans. Refer to the section on future plans on page 72.

DON'T FORGET

Je suis en train de + infinitive means 'I am in the middle of doing' something. It is a fancy phrase that you could use in different contexts.

ACTIVITY: THE EXAMS – LES EXAMENS

Now look at the different types of tasks that you might have to do as part of your exams. Can you work out what they mean in English? You could try to guess which subject(s) each phrase refers to.

1. J'ai des examens écrits et oraux.

2. Je dois passer des examens d'écoute.

3. Je dois lire des textes.

4. Je dois faire des présentations.

5. Je dois répondre aux questions.

6. Il faut rédiger des dissertations.

7. Il faut faire des expériences.

8. Il faut faire de l'arithmétique.

9. Il faut cuisiner un repas.

10. Je dois jouer de la guitare/Je dois chanter.

11. Je dois dessiner des images.

12. Je dois faire du bricolage.

13. Il faut résoudre des problèmes.

14. Il faut pratiquer du sport.

15. Il faut travailler à l'ordinateur.

⚙ ACTIVITY: PREPARATIONS – LES PRÉPARATIONS

What preparation do you do for your different exams? Match the French phrases to the English translations:

1. J'assiste aux cours	A. I learn useful words and definitions off by heart
2. Je m'entraîne à l'examen de français	B. I do research
3. Je révise en ligne	C. I spend a lot of time doing revision at home
4. J'utilise des sites pour la révision sur Internet	D. I go to extra classes
5. Je fais de la recherche	E. I attend lessons
6. Je lis mes notes	F. I practise for the French exam
7. J'apprends des mots utiles et les définitions par cœur	G. I do revision online
8. Je passe beaucoup de temps à réviser chez moi	H. I read my notes
9. Je vais aux cours supplémentaires	I. If there are things I don't understand, I ask my teacher to explain
10. J'ai un emploi du temps pour réviser	J. I have a revision timetable
11. S'il y a des choses que je ne comprends pas, je demande à mon prof de m'expliquer	K. I use websites to do revision

ONLINE TEST

For more false friends try the test at www.brightredbooks.net/N5French

ONLINE

Check out the French Exam Skills page to prepare yourself ahead of your National 5 examination: www.brightredbooks.net/N5French

THINGS TO DO AND THINK ABOUT

Look back at the phrases above. Try to think of three further sentences in French about things you do to prepare for exams. You could refer back to the sections on leisure and healthy living and use some phrases from there to help you out.

PREPARING FOR EXAMS 2 – SE PREPARER AUX EXAMENS

 **ACTIVITY** THE PRESSURE OF EXAMS – LA PRESSION DES EXAMENS

Read the following texts and then answer the questions below.

Benjamin

En ce moment j'étudie pour mes examens. Je trouve qu'il y a beaucoup de pression et mes parents sont toujours sur mon dos. C'est vraiment difficile car je ne suis pas très travailleur et je préférerais passer mon temps à surfer le net ou à jouer aux jeux en ligne. Pour moi, il est important de trouver l'équilibre entre les études et les loisirs pourtant mes parents ne sont pas d'accord. Ils disent que je dois étudier pendant des heures sans faire de pause, mais je trouve les révisions insupportables et vraiment ennuyeuses. Après avoir passé mes examens, j'ai envie de quitter le lycée et de trouver un emploi. Je n'ai pas l'intention de continuer mes études au lycée.

Laure

Cette année, je me prépare pour mes examens. Je sais que c'est ma responsabilité parce que j'ai l'intention de continuer mes études à la fac, donc je dois réussir à mes examens. Ça peut être stressant mais je sais que ce n'est que pour quelques mois. Je ne sors pas assez souvent avec mes amis car je me consacre à mes études. Je sais qu'il est important de bien dormir, de faire des pauses et de bien manger car on peut mieux se concentrer si on se sent bien. Mes parents me soutiennent et ils savent que je fais de mon mieux.

1. Who is not coping well with the pressure of exams?

2. Who is taking responsibility for their exams?

3. Who is working hard?

4. Who would prefer to be on the computer instead of studying?

5. Whose parents are very supportive?

6. Whose parents are putting them under a lot of pressure?

7. Who is not going to continue studying?

8. Who wants to go to university?

9. Who doesn't see their friends much?

10. Who studies for hours without taking a break?

11. Who thinks that being healthy will help them to concentrate?

contd

Now find the French for the following in the texts:

1. There is a lot of pressure.
2. It's my responsibility.
3. My parents are always on my back.
4. I have to pass my exams.
5. I would prefer to spend my time ...
6. To find the balance between studies and leisure ...
7. Exams are unbearable.
8. It can be stressful.
9. I devote myself to my studies.
10. I don't intend to continue.
11. You can concentrate better if you feel well.
12. I am doing my best.

THINGS TO DO AND THINK ABOUT

There may be some phrases in the text that you may wish to use in your Performance. Write a paragraph about:

- your ambitions to do well in your exams
- the exams you are working towards
- what exactly you have to do
- how you prepare for your exams
- whether you think you are coping well with the pressure.

VIDEO LINK

Watch the clip 'Jobs, study and qualifications' and try out the listening comprehension exercise at the end: www.brightredbooks.net/N5French

ONLINE TEST

Try the 'Preparing for exams' test at www.brightredbooks.net/N5French

DON'T FORGET

Après avoir and *après être* are known as the **perfect infinitive** and they translate as 'after having done something', for example *après avoir passé mes examens* means 'after having sat my exams'. They are followed by the past participle and the agreement rules for *être* verbs apply.

DIFFERENT EDUCATION SYSTEMS – LES SYSTÈMES SCOLAIRES DIFFÉRENTS

The Scottish education system is very different from systems in other countries.

ONLINE

To find out more about Francophone countries, why not do some research using the sites on the BrightRED Digital Zone.

DON'T FORGET

It is very important that you revise French numbers regularly. In this topic about school, you need to recognise and understand different numbers in the context of the number of pupils at school and time. Make sure you spend lots of time revising numbers!

ONLINE TEST

Head to www.brightredbooks.net/N5French and take the test on different education systems.

⚙ ACTIVITY: THE SCHOOL SYSTEM – LE SYSTÈME SCOLAIRE

Read the following texts about two young people talking about their school system then answer the questions in the table.

Isabelle

Je vais au lycée à Québec. C'est un lycée moyen avec neuf cent cinquante élèves. Le bâtiment est moderne et bien équipé. Je vais au lycée à vélo. Les cours commencent à huit heures quinze et finissent à quatorze heures quarante. Il y a quatre cours par jour et chaque cours dure une heure et quart. Il y a une récré à dix heures cinquante-cinq et le déjeuner est à midi trente. Le déjeuner dure cinquante minutes et je mange à la cantine avec mes amis. La nourriture est très saine et à mon avis, il y a un bon choix. J'étudie huit matières et ma matière préférée, c'est le dessin. Il y a vingt-cinq élèves dans ma classe et il faut aller aux salles de classe différentes, par exemple, il y a des labos et des salles d'informatique. J'aime les profs au lycée car ils sont compréhensifs et patients. Au lycée, on ne doit pas porter l'uniforme, ce qui je pense est une mauvaise idée. Je préférerais porter l'uniforme car il est cher d'acheter des vêtements différents pour être à la mode au lycée tous les jours. Ce que j'aime le plus c'est qui je peux passer du temps avec mes amis, on bavarde et on rigole pendant le déjeuner. Par contre, ce que je n'aime pas c'est qu'il n'y a pas assez de bancs dans la cour de récré.

Pierre

Mon lycée se trouve à Dakar au Sénégal. C'est un grand lycée avec mille huit cent élèves. C'est un vieux bâtiment démodé. Je vais au lycée à pied donc je dois me lever très tôt le matin car les cours commencent à 8 heures. Les cours finissent à dix-sept heures. Il y a quatre cours par jour et chaque cours dure deux heures. Nous avons une récré qui dure une demi-heure et nous avons une heure pour le déjeuner à midi. Normalement je vais chez moi pour manger le déjeuner car la cantine est trop chère. J'étudie neuf matières et ma matière préférée, c'est la géographie. Il y a quarante-sept élèves dans ma classe et nous restons dans la même salle de classe toute la journée. Il y a un terrain de foot et un terrain de basket. Les profs sont abordables et ils respectent les élèves. Le règlement au lycée est très strict, par exemple on n'a pas le droit d'utiliser des portables ou de parler pendant les cours. Ce que j'aime le plus, c'est qu'il ne faut pas porter l'uniforme donc je me sens confortable. Ce que je n'aime pas, c'est qu'il n'y a pas assez d'ordinateurs.

Questions	Isabelle	Pierre	Mélanie (listening)
Where is the school?			
What size is it?			
How many pupils are there?			
What is the building like?			
How do they get to school?			
What time do lessons start and finish?			
How many classes do they have per day and how long does each class last?			
What time is lunch?			
How long is the lunch break?			

contd

Where do they eat lunch?			
What is their opinion of the canteen?			
How many subjects do they study?			
What is their favourite subject?			
How many pupils are there in their classes?			
What facilities are there?			
What do they say about their teachers?			
Do they wear a uniform?			
What is their opinion of wearing a uniform?			
What do they like about school?			
What do they not like about school?			

ACTIVITY: MÉLANIE'S SCHOOL

Now that you have read about Isabelle's and Pierre's schools, listen to Mélanie describe her school. Use the same table as before and complete as many details as possible by listening out for key words.

ACTIVITY: THE SCHOOL SYSTEM IN SCOTLAND – LE SYSTÈME SCOLAIRE EN ÉCOSSE

Now that you have read about different school systems in different French speaking countries, it would also be a good idea to think about how these schools differ from Scottish schools. Listen to Nicolas describing the school system in Scotland. Here are some tips:

- Read the information that you are required to find (the questions/ the table) and underline key words
- Try to predict what you are going to hear (numbers/ places/ people/ activities/ times etc.)
- Think about the vocabulary that you might hear and predict the key words that you need to listen out for (bâtiment/élèves / commencent/ finissent/profs/ etc.)
- The first time you listen to the text, try to answer as many of the questions as you can but don't worry if you don't get every piece of information

- Put a star or a tick beside the questions that you didn't complete so the second time you listen to the text, you know what questions and information to focus on
- The third time you listen to the text should be your chance to fill in any remaining gaps and check the answers that you have written down are correct
- Make sure to always check your answers carefully – do they actually answer the questions?
- Don't leave any blanks, do your best to make an intelligent guess!

Questions:

1. Where is the school that Nicholas visited?
2. What size is it?
3. How many pupils are there in the school?
4. What is the building like?
5. When do classes start and finish?
6. What time is lunch?
7. What do most pupils do at lunch time?
8. How many subjects do pupils study?
9. How many pupils are in each class?
10. What does he say about pupils wearing uniform?
11. What does Nicolas like about Scottish schools?
12. What does Nicolas dislike about Scottish schools?

THINGS TO DO AND THINK ABOUT

Using the reading and listening texts in this section as a guide for structure and content, write as much as you can about your school. You can select appropriate vocabulary from the reading texts and the listening transcripts and change the key information to describe your school. You can use this text as part of your Performance.

- Where is your school?
- What is your school like?
- What size is your school?
- What time do lessons start and finish?
- How many lessons are there per day?
- How long do lessons last?
- How many pupils are in each class?
- Do you have to wear uniform?
- What is your opinion of wearing uniform?
- What do you like about your school system?
- What do you dislike about your school system?

IMPROVING EDUCATION SYSTEMS – AMÉLIORER LES SYSTÈMES SCOLAIRES

HOW CAN YOU IMPROVE YOUR EDUCATION SYSTEM? – COMMENT EST-CE QU'ON PEUT AMÉLIORER SON SYSTÈME SCOLAIRE?

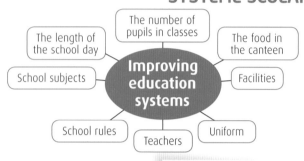

We have looked at the education systems in different countries. Was there anything that you liked about the other systems that you would like to happen in your school? Think about the following:

 **ACTIVITY** MY PREFERENCES AT SCHOOL – MES PRÉFÉRENCES AU LYCÉE

Have a look at the following phrases, which describe some common complaints about schools and how they would ideally be. Translate them into English then try to match the complaints to the correct ideal situation.

Common complaints	Ideal situation
Les cours sont ennuyeux.	Je voudrais porter ce que je veux au lycée.
Je trouve les matières traditionnelles assez monotones.	Je préférerais une récré d'une demi-heure.
Il y a trente élèves dans ma classe.	J'aimerais avoir plus d'équipements sportifs.
Les cours commencent à neuf heures.	Je voudrais avoir deux heures pour le déjeuner.
Les cours finissent à trois heures et demie.	Je voudrais des cours intéressants et amusants.
Nous avons quarante-cinq minutes pour le déjeuner.	Je préfère être dans une classe de vingt élèves.
On a une récré de quinze minutes.	Je voudrais étudier des matières plus dynamiques et modernes comme la danse.
C'est trop cher et il n'y a pas de choix à la cantine.	J'aimerais avoir plus de liberté au lycée.
Il n'y a pas assez d'ordinateurs.	Je voudrais finir à une heure.
Il n'y a pas assez d'équipements sportifs.	Je voudrais commencer à onze heures.
La bibliothèque est petite et il n'y a pas assez de choix de livres.	Je voudrais avoir des plats moins chers et plus de choix à la cantine.
Le règlement est trop strict.	Je préfère les profs qui sont détendus.
Les élèves n'ont pas beaucoup de liberté.	J'aimerais avoir plus de salles d'informatique.
Il faut porter un uniforme, ce qui est affreux.	J'aimerais moins de règles au lycée.
On ne doit pas porter d'uniforme.	J'aimerais avoir des profs qui ne donneraient jamais de devoirs.
Mes profs sont très sévères.	J'aimerais une grande bibliothèque avec un bon choix de livres.
Les profs nous donnent trop de devoirs.	Je voudrais porter l'uniforme car tout le monde est égal.

ACTIVITY: THE RULES – LE RÈGLEMENT

Let's focus more closely on the rules in school that you would like to change and the reasons why. Listen to the following people talking about which rules they would like to change at their school and why. Fill in the gaps using the words in the boxes below. Here are some tips to help you complete this listening task:

- Read through the texts first to get an idea of what the subject matter is and use your dictionary to look up any new words you don't recognise.

- Try to predict what you might hear by guessing in advance what words might fit into the blanks.

- Listen to the text as many times as you need to until all the gaps have been filled in.

Antoine

A mon avis, mon lycée est un _____ lycée. Il y a trop de _____ et il faut les suivre. Pendant les cours on doit _____ le prof et on n'a pas le droit de _____ ou de manger. En plus, on n'a pas le droit d'utiliser son _____ au lycée, même pendant la récré ou l'heure du déjeuner. Je pense que le règlement, ce n'est pas _____.

boire   mauvais   juste   portable   écouter   règles

Bernadette

Au lycée, il faut porter l'uniforme. Certains pensent que c'est une _____ idée car tout le monde se _____ et donc il n'y a pas d'_____. Je pense que l'uniforme, c'est une bonne idée. Ça ne _____ pas cher et on ne peut pas remarquer les différences _____ entre les élèves. En plus, on ne _____ pas de temps à décider quoi porter chaque matin.

coûte   individualité   perd   sociales   ressemble   mauvaise

Stéphanie

Mon lycée idéal serait assez petit et très moderne. Il n'y aurait que quinze _____ dans chaque classe et les profs seraient vraiment gentils et _____. Ils ne nous donneraient jamais de _____. Les cours commenceraient à dix heures et finiraient à une heure. On étudierait des matières intéressantes et _____. On aurait le droit d'utiliser son _____ et son iPad pendant les cours. La nourriture à la cantine serait _____ et pas chère. Il n'y aurait pas d'uniforme et on aurait le droit de porter ce qu'on veut.

serviables   élèves   portable   devoirs   saine   utiles

What do you notice about Stéphanie's text? Do you recognise the tense she is using to describe her ideal school? Think back to the section when you described your ideal parents (pages 16–17) or your ideal place to live (pages 40–5). Can you think of any other things that you would like to change about your school or education system? Try to use the conditional tense to talk about your ideal school.

DON'T FORGET

The conditional tense is used to describe what something *would be* or what someone *would do*. Refer to page 88 to revise the conditional tense.

ONLINE

Have a look at the 'About France' link to read about how the school system works in France and jot down anything you'd like to see in Scotland: www.brightredbooks.net/N5French

ONLINE TEST

Take the 'Improving education systems' test at www.brightredbooks.net/N5French

THINGS TO DO AND THINK ABOUT

Now write a paragraph describing what happens at your school and what you would like to change. Use the phrases in this section to help you or try to make up your own. Think about the school day, your subjects, teachers, school rules, facilities, canteen and extra-curricular activities. Try to include a couple of phrases using the conditional tense. You may wish to use this paragraph as part of your Performance.

EMPLOYABILITY

DIFFERENT JOBS – LES EMPLOIS DIFFÉRENTS

This chapter on employability is all about the world of work. We'll start by revising different types of jobs.

DON'T FORGET

Many job names in French change depending on gender, for example *coiffeur* is masculine and *coiffeuse* is feminine. If you are unsure of the feminine form of different jobs, use your dictionary to check.

ONLINE TEST

Take the online test to revise different jobs at www.brightredbooks/N5French

ONLINE

Look at the vocabulary list online for more professions: www.brightredbooks.net/N5French

DON'T FORGET

Je suis infirmier means 'I am a nurse': in French you *do not* include the **indefinite article** (a).

Future jobs:
- Électricien(e)
- Ingénieur(e)
- Pharmacien(ne)
- Fermier/fermière
- Coiffeur/coiffeuse
- Infirmier/infirmière

ACTIVITY: WHERE DO YOU WORK? – OÙ TRAVAILLES-TU?

Look at the following phrases about places of work. Can you match the phrases to the correct job or jobs that follow?

1. Je travaille dans un hôpital.
2. Je travaille dans un lycée.
3. Je travaille dans une école primaire.
4. Je travaille dans un restaurant.
5. Je travaille dans un garage.
6. Je travaille dans un commissariat.
7. Je travaille dans un bureau.
8. Je travaille dans un magasin.

A. Je suis infirmier.
B. Je suis vendeur.
C. Je suis agent de police.
D. Je suis serveur.
E. Je suis secrétaire.
F. Je suis instituteur
G. Je suis professeur.
H. Je suis mécanicien.

 **ACTIVITY: QUALITIES FOR DIFFERENT JOBS – LES QUALITÉS POUR LES EMPLOIS DIFFÉRENTS**

Different jobs require different qualities and skills, for example to be a teacher you need to be patient, organised and have good communication skills.

Have a look at the following phrases about skills and list them under the jobs shown that require that skill. There might be some skills that match more than one job. Use your dictionary to work out the meanings of any unfamiliar vocabulary.

Pharmacien(ne)   Journaliste   Pompier   Réceptionniste

1. Il faut être travailleur et en bonne forme.
2. On doit être motivé et déterminé.
3. Il faut être organisé et flexible.
4. On doit aimer travailler en équipe.
5. Il faut avoir de l'énergie et de l'enthousiasme.
6. Il faut avoir de bonnes notes et un diplôme.
7. On doit avoir la capacité de travailler sous la pression.
8. Il faut avoir une connaissance des ordinateurs.
9. On doit avoir une bonne mémoire.
10. On doit savoir taper rapidement.
11. Il faut savoir bien communiquer avec les autres.
12. C'est utile si on sait parler une langue étrangère.

 DON'T FORGET

On doit and *il faut* are always followed by the infinitive. *On doit* comes from the modal verb *devoir*, and *savoir* is another modal verb meaning 'to know how to'. To revise modal verbs, look at pages 26–7.

VIDEO LINK

Check out the clips about the world of work: www.brightredbooks.net/N5French

 **ACTIVITY: REVISION – LA RÉVISION**

1. Choose three different jobs and write down in French what skills you need for them using the vocabulary you have just learned.

2. Now translate the following paragraphs into English using all of the vocabulary from this section. Use a dictionary to help you work out the meaning of any unfamiliar language. Don't forget to make links to English where possible!

(a) Je voudrais être médecin. Il faut réussir à mes examens et je dois obtenir de bonnes notes. Pour être médecin on doit avoir de la patience, savoir bien communiquer avec les gens malades et avoir la capacité de travailler sous la pression.

(b) J'aimerais être musicienne. On doit être créatif et avoir beaucoup de talent, d'enthousiasme et d'énergie. J'aimerais savoir parler une langue étrangère car c'est utile si on a l'occasion de voyager autour du monde.

(c) À l'avenir, je voudrais devenir vétérinaire. On doit être travailleur, poli et organisé. Il faut savoir bien communiquer avec les autres et on doit adorer les animaux. En plus, il est important d'avoir une bonne mémoire.

(d) À l'avenir, j'aimerais être hôtesse de l'air. Il faut être en forme, sociable et poli. Je voudrais voyager autour du monde et j'habiterai peut-être à l'étranger. On doit travailler en équipe et aimer travailler avec le public.

 DON'T FORGET

Some of the verbs are in the future and conditional tenses. To revise these tenses, refer to page 88.

 THINGS TO DO AND THINK ABOUT

Using the vocabulary in this section choose a job that you would like to do in the future and write a paragraph about the qualities you need to have to do this job successfully. You will be able to add to this when we get to the section on future plans and may wish to use this as part of your Performance. You should also refer to the section on writing to help you.

PART-TIME JOBS – LES PETITS BOULOTS 1

You might already have a part-time job or you might be considering getting one to earn some money. Let's brainstorm some of the jobs you could do. Can you add any others?

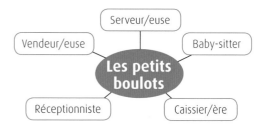

Serveur/euse
Vendeur/euse
Baby-sitter
Les petits boulots
Réceptionniste
Caissier/ère

⚙ ACTIVITY: MY PART-TIME JOB – MON PETIT BOULOT

Read the following sentences and find out where each person works and what jobs they do.

1. Je travaille dans un café, je suis serveur.

2. Je travaille dans un hôtel, je suis réceptionniste.

3. Je travaille dans un magasin, je suis vendeuse/vendeur.

4. Je travaille dans un supermarché, je suis caissier.

5. Je m'occupe des enfants de mes voisins, je suis baby-sitter.

APPLYING FOR A PART-TIME JOB – POSER SA CANDIDATURE POUR UN POSTE

If you are thinking of applying for a part-time job, it would be very useful to put together a CV. Use the links listed to help you write a CV in French. Some of the vocabulary that you will need to write a CV can also be used in the Writing section of your exam. Refer to the chapter on writing (pp 84–95) to help you.

You may also want to write a cover letter/email in French.

ONLINE

Head online and check out the links to help you write a CV in French: www.brightredbooks.net/N5French

ONLINE

Look at the links online to help you write a cover letter/email in French: www.brightredbooks.net/N5French

ONLINE

For further practice in reading and working out the meaning of job adverts, refer to the website links in the BrightRED Digital Zone.

⚙ ACTIVITY: JOB ADVERTS – LES OFFRES D'EMPLOI

Skim read the following job adverts and try to pick out some key points: what the job is, the hours, the pay and anything else you can understand. Then answer these questions:

1. Which job would you apply for and why?

2. Which job would you not apply for and why?

Advert A

Vous aimez la nourriture? Vous êtes travailleur et motivé? Nous offrons la possibilité de travailler comme serveur/serveuse dans notre petit restaurant familial. Il faut être âgé de plus de 16 ans. Nous proposons un travail de dix heures par semaine. Les repas sont inclus et vous gagnerez sept euros par heure et des pourboires. Vous devez travailler le soir. Veuillez nous contacter au 02 72 54 46 30.

Advert B

Nous proposons un stage professionnel dans un salon de coiffeur. C'est l'occasion idéale d'apprendre les compétences nécessaires pour devenir coiffeur. Vous devez être poli, serviable et enthousiaste. Il faut organiser les rendez-vous des clients, laver les cheveux des clients et travailler à la caisse. Une expérience préalable n'est pas nécessaire. Vous devrez travailler le samedi de neuf heures du matin à cinq heures du soir. Vous gagnerez six euros vingt-cinq de l'heure. Veuillez appeler 01 72 41 25 86.

contd

Advert C

Vous aimez être en plein air? Nous recherchons des jeunes qui peuvent travailler dans les jardins publics. Vous devez être âgé de 13 à 16 ans et il faut être énergique, honnête et ponctuel. Il faut arroser les plantes et les fleurs. Nous proposons un travail d'une heure après les cours. Vous devez avoir la permission des parents. Vous pourrez travailler près de chez vous et vous gagnerez trente-cinq euros par semaine. Pour plus de renseignements, veuillez appeler 02 72 15 34 67.

 **ACTIVITY:** WHAT DO YOU DO AT WORK? – QU'EST-CE QUE TU FAIS AU TRAVAIL?

If you already have a part-time job, or for the sake of the Writing exam you are pretending to have a part-time job, you might want to say what your responsibilities and duties are at work.

Read the following phrases and decide which job is being described. Some phrases can be used for more than one job. Don't forget to use your dictionary to look up the meaning of any unfamiliar vocabulary. The jobs being described are:

réceptionniste, caissier/caissière, vendeur/vendeuse, baby-sitter, serveur/serveuse

1. Je dois ranger les vêtements.

2. Il faut servir les clients.

3. Il faut travailler avec le public.

4. Je dois manipuler de l'argent.

5. Je dois m'occuper des enfants et ranger la maison.

6. Je dois vendre des boissons, des magazines et des chips.

7. Il faut classer les documents.

8. Il faut répondre au téléphone.

9. Je dois préparer les sandwichs, le thé et le café.

10. Je dois prendre les réservations.

11. Il faut travailler à l'ordinateur.

12. Je dois aider les enfants avec leurs devoirs.

 ONLINE TEST

Test how well you have learned about part-time jobs at www.brightredbooks.net/N5French.

 **ACTIVITY:** WHEN DO YOU WORK? – QUAND EST-CE QUE TU TRAVAILLES?

Listen to the people on the audio track talking about when they work and note down:

1. the days that they work
2. the hours they do
3. how much they earn per hour
4. how they get to work.

If you get stuck, read the transcripts below:

A. Je travaille le lundi après-midi et le mercredi soir. Je fais huit heures par semaine et je gagne cinq euros quatre-vingts par heure. Je vais au travail en bus et en train.

B. Je travaille le samedi de neuf heures du matin à cinq heures du soir et le dimanche du midi à quatre heures de l'après-midi. Je fais douze heures par semaine et je gagne six euros trente-cinq de l'heure. Je vais au travail en voiture.

C. Je travaille le jeudi après l'école et le vendredi soir. Je fais six heures par semaine et je gagne sept euros quinze par heure. Je vais au travail à vélo.

D. Je travaille deux fois par semaine: le dimanche matin et le mardi après-midi. Je fais cinq heures par semaine et je gagne six euros quatre-vingt-quinze par heure. Je vais au travail à pied.

 THINGS TO DO AND THINK ABOUT

This is a chance for you to revise basic vocabulary such as days of the week, time phrases and numbers. Try drawing a mind map and brainstorming as much vocabulary as possible under these headings:

- days of the week
- months of the year
- time phrases (every month, week, fortnight, sometimes, often, rarely etc.)
- numbers.

PART-TIME JOBS – LES PETITS BOULOTS 2

DON'T FORGET

Even if you don't have a part-time job, you need to know how to write about having one so get your thinking cap on and make one up!

OPINIONS OF PART-TIME JOBS – LES OPINIONS DES PETITS BOULOTS

Now that you have learned how to say where you work, what job you do, what tasks you do at work, when you work, how much you earn and how you get to work, you should try to give your opinion of your part-time job. It is not enough to say that you like or dislike your job; you must give reasons for your opinions.

You can start with:

- J'adore mon petit boulot car ...
- J'aime mon travail parce que ...
- Je n'aime pas mon petit boulot car ...
- Je déteste mon travail parce que ...

Then add the adjective to describe your job (if you don't know the meanings of these adjectives, use your dictionary to look them up):

... c'est ...

- intéressant
- amusant
- ennuyeux
- affreux
- génial
- facile
- nul
- fatigant
- fantastique
- varié
- difficile
- bien/mal-payé

 ACTIVITY: OPINIONS – LES OPINIONS

These are very basic opinions and reasons so let's learn some fancier phrases.

Match the French to the English phrases and then decide if the opinion is positive or negative. Try to make links to English words to work out what the phrases mean. If there is still language you don't understand, use your dictionary to look up the meaning.

1. Les clients sont sympas	A. My boss is patient and helpful
2. J'aime travailler en équipe	B. I have the chance to learn things
3. Je peux rencontrer de nouvelles personnes	C. The customers are rude and impatient
4. Mes collègues sont énervants	D. I don't have time to study
5. J'ai beaucoup de choses à faire	E. Time passes quickly
6. Je suis très occupé(e)	F. My colleagues are annoying
7. Je n'ai pas le temps d'étudier	G. I like having responsibility
8. Je peux gagner de l'argent pour financer mes études	H. I have to wear a uniform and it is not comfortable
9. Je peux acquérir de l'expérience	I. The customers are nice
10. J'aime avoir de la responsabilité	J. My boss is too strict
11. J'ai l'occasion d'apprendre des choses	K. The hours are long
12. Je ne m'ennuie jamais	L. I have a lot of things to do
13. Mon patron est patient et serviable	M. I can meet new people
14. Mon patron est trop sévère	N. I like working in a team
15. Les clients sont impolis et impatients	O. I don't have enough free time

contd

16.	Je n'ai pas assez de temps libre	P.	I have to work alone, which is boring
17.	Le temps passe vite	Q.	I never get bored
18.	Il faut me lever tôt	R.	I'm very busy
19.	Je dois porter l'uniforme et ce n'est pas confortable	S.	I have to get up early
20.	Les heures sont longues	T.	I can gain experience
21.	Je dois travailler seul, ce qui est ennuyeux	U.	I can earn money to pay for my studies

 **ACTIVITY:** REVISION – LA RÉVISION

Translate the following paragraphs into English. This is good training for Higher French. If there are sections you are unsure of, try to focus on picking out the main points from the texts. Use a dictionary to look up any unfamiliar vocabulary.

1. Je suis serveuse dans un café au centre-ville. Je dois préparer le thé et le café et servir les clients. Je travaille trois fois par semaine et je gagne cinq euros soixante-dix par heure. J'aime mon travail parce que c'est facile et amusant. Je suis toujours très occupée donc le temps passe vite. En plus, mon patron est patient et mes collègues sont serviables. Je ne m'ennuie jamais, ce qui est génial!

2. Je travaille comme vendeur dans un magasin de vêtements. Je dois aider les clients, ranger le magasin et manipuler de l'argent. Ce que j'aime le plus, c'est que j'ai des réductions et les clients sont polis. Pourtant, parfois, je déteste mon boulot parce que mon patron est trop sévère et impatient. En plus, je dois travailler quatre fois par semaine donc je n'ai pas assez de temps libre. Finalement, mon petit-boulot est mal payé, je ne gagne que cinq euros vingt par heure.

3. Je suis réceptionniste dans un hôtel au bord de la mer. Je dois répondre au téléphone, résoudre les problèmes et prendre les réservations. Je travaille tous les samedis et je fais neuf heures par semaine. C'est bien payé car je gagne sept euros quarante par heure. C'est génial car on me donne des pourboires aussi. Mon patron est très sympa et mes collègues sont gentils.

 ACTIVITY: STUDYING AND WORKING – ÉTUDIER ET TRAVAILLER

If you go to college or university you might decide to find a part-time job to help subsidise your studies. There are advantages and disadvantages of having a part-time job at the same time as studying. Listen to the audio track to hear four people talking about having a part-time job and studying. Can you note down any advantages and disadvantages they mention?

THINGS TO DO AND THINK ABOUT

Write a paragraph about your part-time job. Even if you don't have a part-time job, pretend that you do! Use the language you have learned in this section to help you. Try to include the following:

- where you work
- what you do
- when you work
- how many hours you work
- how much you earn
- how you get to work
- your opinion of your part-time job
- reasons for your opinion
- any advantages or disadvantages there may be to having a part-time job and studying at the same time.

 DON'T FORGET

Refer to the section on describing family members on pages 8–9 if you want to describe your boss or colleagues.

ONLINE TEST

Test how well you have learned about part-time jobs at www.brightredbooks.net/N5French

 ONLINE

Have a look at the page about Stanislas and Layla to hear about their part-time jobs and career goals: www.brightredbooks.net/N5French

WORK EXPERIENCE – MON STAGE EN ENTREPRISE

In this section you will learn to describe any work experience you have done. Although you may not have done any work experience yet, you need to be able to write about it in the Writing section of your exam, so use your imagination. This section will also give you the opportunity to revise the perfect and imperfect tenses, which are both used to describe actions completed in the past.

Let's start by thinking of where you might have done your work experience. Can you think of any other examples?

ACTIVITY MY WORK EXPERIENCE – MON STAGE EN ENTREPRISE

Read the following texts about different people's work experiences. Can you complete the table on page 67?

Try to make links to English to work out what any unfamiliar vocabulary means. Use your dictionary to look up other unfamiliar language.

Marion

J'ai travaillé dans un magasin de sport comme vendeuse. Je commençais à huit heures et demie et je finissais à seize heures. Je devais servir les clients et je travaillais à la caisse. J'ai beaucoup aimé le contact avec le public. Pourtant je n'ai pas aimé le patron car il était désagréable. A mon avis, mon stage était une bonne expérience car c'était varié.

Stéphane

Pendant mon stage en entreprise, j'ai travaillé dans un fast-food. Je commençais à dix heures du matin et je finissais à dix-neuf heures. Je devais préparer les frites et les hamburgers. Ce que j'ai aimé le plus, c'était le travail en équipe. Par contre, j'ai trouvé la journée très longue car à la fin de la journée, j'étais très fatigué. Je pense que mon stage était une mauvaise expérience car c'était monotone.

Laure

J'ai travaillé dans un salon de coiffure. Je commençais à neuf heures et je finissais à dix-huit heures. Pendant mon stage, je devais repondre au téléphone et je devais accuellir les clients. Je préparais le café pour les clients et je rangerais le salon. J'ai aimé le travail car les clients étaient gentils et mon patron était patient et compréhensif. Pourtant, c'était une longue journée et il n'y avait pas beaucoup de pauses pour le personnel. En somme, mon stage était une bonne expérience car c'était facile.

contd

Marcus

Pendant mon stage, j'ai travaillé dans un bureau d'une grande entreprise. Je commençais à neuf heures et je finissais à dix-sept heures trente. Je devais classer les documents et envoyer des emails. J'ai aimé le travail car je m'entendais bien avec mes collègues et j'ai beaucoup appris. En revanche je n'ai pas aimé travailler seul. A mon avis, mon stage était une bonne expérience car c'était intéressant.

	Where did they work?	When did they start?	When did they finish?	What did they do?	What did they like?	What did they not like?	Overall opinion
Marion							
Stéphane							
Laure							
Marcus							

GRAMMAR: THE PERFECT TENSE – LE PASSÉ COMPOSÉ

Look at the reading activity text again. You will notice that each person's work experience is being discussed in the **past tense**. Two tenses are being used, the perfect (*le passé composé*) and the imperfect (*l'imparfait*). To revise the imperfect tense refer to page 47.

This is a great opportunity to revise when the perfect tense is used and how it is formed.

The perfect tense is used to describe a past completed action. It is made up of three parts:

the subject (person/thing doing the verb) + *correct part of avoir/être* (auxiliary verb) + *past participle*

For example: *J'ai joué* – I have played, *Je suis allée* – I have gone

THE PERFECT TENSE WITH AVOIR

1. Let's start with verbs that take avoir in the perfect tense. First, we will revise avoir:

avoir – to have			
j'ai	I have	on a	we have
tu as	you have	nous avons	we have
il a	he has	vous avez	you (plural) have
elle a	she has	ils ont –	they have
		elles ont	they have

2. Now add the **past participle**. The past participle is the 'past part' of the verb. In English we usually add 'ed' to the end of the verb to form the past participle, for example played, talked.

- To form the past participle of an 'er' verb chop off the 'er' and add '<u>é</u>', for example
  regarder – regard<u>é</u>
  J'ai regardé – I have watched

- To form the past participle of an 'ir' verb chop off the 'ir' and add '<u>i</u>', for example
  finir – fin<u>i</u>
  J'ai fini – I have finished

- To form the past participle of an 're' verb chop off the 're' and add 'u', for example
  vendre – vend<u>u</u>
  J'ai vendu – I have sold

DON'T FORGET

In your writing, try to use conjunctions, such as *pourtant* and *en somme*, to help structure your writing. Can you think of any more?

ONLINE

For more information about the perfect tense, have a look at the links: www.brightredbooks.net/N5French

ONLINE TEST

Take the test 'Work experience – Mon stage en entreprise' at www.brightredbooks.net/N5French

DON'T FORGET

Let's revise **subject pronouns**:
je	I
tu	you (informal singular)
il	he
elle	she
on	we
nous	we
vous	you (plural/formal)
ils	they
elles	they (feminine)

THINGS TO DO AND THINK ABOUT

Before revising the perfect tense, make sure you know the irregular verbs avoir and être in the present tense.

MORE ON THE PERFECT TENSE – LE PASSÉ COMPOSE – ENCORE!

THE PERFECT TENSE WITH IRREGULAR PAST PARTICIPLES

DON'T FORGET

Avoir is still used as the auxiliary/helping verb with these irregular past participles.

DON'T FORGET

To check the past participle of an irregular verb, use the verb tables in your dictionary.

You have learned how to form regular past participles as these follow a pattern. However, in English we don't always follow the usual pattern of adding 'ed' to the end of the verb: for instance we don't say 'I have doed', we say 'I have done'. In French, just like in English, there are some **irregular past participles** that you will need to learn off by heart. Have a look at this list:

Infinitive	Past participle	Example using 'je'	English meaning
boire – to drink	bu	J'ai bu	I drank/have drunk
lire – to read	lu	J'ai lu	I read/have read
voir – to see	vu	J'ai vu	I saw/have seen
savoir – to know	su	J'ai su	I knew/have known
devoir – to have to	dû	J'ai dû	I had to/have had to
pouvoir – to be able to	pu	J'ai pu	I was able to/have been able to
vouloir – to want to	voulu	J'ai voulu	I wanted to/have wanted to
recevoir – to receive	reçu	J'ai reçu	I received/have received
prendre – to take	pris	J'ai pris	I took/have taken
apprendre – to learn	appris	J'ai appris	I learned/have learned
comprendre – to understand	compris	J'ai compris	I understood/have understood
mettre – to put	mis	J'ai mis	I put/have put
promettre – to promise	promis	J'ai promis	I promised/have promised
conduire – to drive	conduit	J'ai conduit	I drove/have driven
écrire – to write	écrit	J'ai écrit	I wrote/have written
faire – to do/make	fait	J'ai fait	I did/have done
avoir – to have	eu	J'ai eu	I have had/had
être – to be	été	J'ai été	I have been/was

VERBS THAT TAKE ÊTRE IN THE PERFECT TENSE

Some verbs use être as their auxiliary/helping verb instead of avoir. Verbs that take être are usually verbs of motion or indicate a change of state.

The same formula is used: *subject + correct part of être + past participle*

Let's start by revising être:

Etre – to be

je suis	I am
tu es	you are
il est	he is
elle est	she is
on est	we are
nous sommes	we are
vous êtes	you are
ils sont	they are
elles sont	they are

MRS VANDERTRAMP

A good way of remembering verbs that take être is: **MRS VANDERTRAMP**

Infinitive	Past participle	Example using 'je'	English meaning
Monter – to go up	monté	Je suis monté(e)	I went up/have gone up
Rentrer – to go back in	rentré	Je suis rentré(e)	I went back in/have gone back in/returned
Sortir – to go out	sorti	Je suis sorti(e)	I went out/have been out
Venir – to come	venu	Je suis venu(e)	I came/have come
Aller – to go	allé	Je suis allé(e)	I went/have gone
Naître – to be born	né	Je suis né(e)	I was born/have been born
Descendre – to go down	descendu	Je suis descendu(e)	I descended/have gone down
Entrer – to enter	entré	Je suis entré(e)	I entered/have entered
Retourner – to return	retourné	Je suis retourné(e)	I returned/have returned
Tomber – to fall	tombé	Je suis tombé(e)	I fell/have fallen
Rester – to stay	resté	Je suis resté(e)	I stayed/have stayed
Arriver – to arrive	arrivé	Je suis arrivé(e)	I arrived/have arrived
Mourir – to die	mort	Je suis mort(e)	I died/have died
Partir – to leave	parti	Je suis parti(e)	I left/have left

VIDEO LINK

Have a look at the Mrs Vandertramp video at www.brightredbooks.net/N5French

AGREEMENT OF ÊTRE VERBS IN THE PERFECT TENSE

Now let's look at the verb sortir in the perfect tense:

je suis sorti(e)

tu es sorti(e)

il est sorti

elle est sortie

nous sommes sorti(e)s

vous êtes sorti(e)s

ils sont sortis

elles sont sorties

If you look carefully, you will notice that the spelling of *sorti* changes for some of the people. Can you work out why?

When you use être in the perfect tense you must change the past participle depending on the person (it must agree!):

- If the person is feminine, add *e* to the past participle.

- If the person is plural, add an *s* to the past participle.

- If the person is feminine and plural, add *es* to the past participle.

ONLINE

Practise the perfect tense using the link online at www.brightredbooks.net/N5French

ONLINE

For more on this, check out the page on the *passé composé* (www.brightredbooks.net/N5French). Go to the grammar section and start with 'The perfect tense for beginners'.

ONLINE TEST

Take this online test to see how well you can form the perfect tense: www.brightredbooks.net/N5French.

THINGS TO DO AND THINK ABOUT

Now that you have revised the perfect tense, write sentences for each of the following in the perfect tense:

- five avoir verbs with regular past participles

- five avoir verbs with irregular past participles

- five être verbs.

WORK EXPERIENCE ACTIVITIES – LES ACTIVITÉS PENDANT UN STAGE

 **ACTIVITY** POSITIVE OR NEGATIVE – POSITIF OU NÉGATIF

Have a look at the following phrases and decide if they are describing something positive or negative about work experience. Put them under the headings *positif* or *négatif*.

1. J'ai dû porter un uniforme, c'était confortable.
2. Il fallait être debout pendant longtemps, c'était fatigant.
3. J'ai passé des heures à travailler à l'ordinateur, c'était monotone.
4. J'ai travaillé dehors, c'était génial.
5. J'ai travaillé avec le public, c'était intéressant.
6. J'ai travaillé en équipe, c'était amusant.
7. J'ai travaillé seul, c'était affreux.
8. J'ai fait l'expérience du commerce, c'était varié.
9. J'ai travaillé dans le domaine du tourisme, c'était fantastique.
10. J'étais responsable de la caisse, je me suis bien amusé(e).
11. Je n'ai rien appris, c'était une perte de temps.
12. J'ai appris à envoyer un fax, c'était utile.

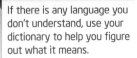 **DON'T FORGET**

If there is any language you don't understand, use your dictionary to help you figure out what it means.

 **ACTIVITY** WHO IS IT? – C'EST QUI?

Listen to the passages about work experience placements on the audio track and answer the questions as best you can. Read the questions first and pick out key words that you think will come up in the text. Listen to the text as many times as you need to in order to answer all the questions.

1. Who worked in a music shop?
2. Who had to wear a uniform?
3. Who learned some new things?
4. Who worked with children?
5. Who went to work by bus?
6. Who met nice people?
7. Who did not work in the evening?
8. Who learned how to operate a till?
9. Who went to work by train?
10. Who worked at the weekend?

ACTIVITY: REVISION – LA RÉVISION

Read about Lucie's work experience and answer the questions which follow. Look at how many marks each questions is worth and make sure that you write enough information to be awarded full marks.

Lucie

J'ai fait mon stage dans une école primaire. J'y suis allée en bus et à pied. Le voyage a duré trente minutes. Je commençais le travail à neuf heures moins le quart et je finissais à quinze heures dix. J'avais une pause de quinze minutes à dix heures et demie et la pause du déjeuner était à treize heures. J'étais chargée d'aider les enfants à lire dans de petits groupes, d'organiser des jeux et d'aider les élèves à faire leur travail. J'ai aussi aidé les profs à ranger la salle de classe et je devais classer les dossiers des professeurs. J'ai appris à bien communiquer avec les enfants et à organiser des activités. Je me suis bien amusée parce que les enfants étaient vraiment amusants et pleins de vie. À mon avis, mon stage était utile et varié. En effet, j'ai décidé de devenir institutrice à l'avenir.

1. Where did Lucie do her work experience? (1)
2. How did she get to her placement? (2)
3. How long did the journey take? (3)
4. What time did she start work? (1)
5. What time did she finish? (1)
6. When were her breaks? (2)
7. What was she responsible for? (5)
8. What did she learn? (2)
9. Did she enjoy the placement? Why? (4)
10. What has she decided to do as a result of her placement? (1)

 VIDEO LINK

Watch the clip 'Qu'est-ce que tu veux faire dans la vie?' to hear about a volunteer work placement and some ideas about what to do in the future: www.brightredbooks. net/N5French

 ONLINE TEST

Take the 'Work experience' test online at www. brightredbooks.net/N5French to see how well you know this topic.

THINGS TO DO AND THINK ABOUT

Now it is your turn to write about your work experience using the vocabulary from each of the activities in this section. Refer to the section on writing (pp 82–95) as well to help you.

To be successful in this task, include all information in the bullet points and check the accuracy of your tenses using the previous activities and any other support materials you have. Make sure that your work makes sense: can you translate every word or have you left any words out? Avoid translating directly from English and use your dictionary to check the gender of nouns as well as your spelling and accents.

- Where did you do your work experience?
- How did you get there?
- What time did you start and finish?
- What did you do? Did you learn anything?
- What did you enjoy and why?
- Is there anything you didn't enjoy?
- What is your overall opinion of your work experience?

MY FUTURE PLANS – MES PROJETS POUR L'AVENIR

We touched briefly on future plans when we looked at the qualities and skills needed for different jobs. Now we are going to go into more depth. Can you think of what we could cover in this section?

Prendre une année sabbatique

Continuer mes études

Mes projets pour l'avenir

Gagner de l'argent

Trouver un emploi

Voyager autour du monde

Travailler dans le commerce

DON'T FORGET

There are two future tenses in French (see the last four phrases): the **near future tense** (*futur proche*) states what you *are going to do* and is formed by: subject + aller + infinitive. The simple future tense explains what you *will* do and is formed by: subject + infinitive/future stem + future ending. To revise these tenses refer to page 88.

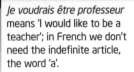

DON'T FORGET

Je voudrais être professeur means 'I would like to be a teacher'; in French we don't need the indefinite article, the word 'a'.

USEFUL VOCABULARY

Here is some useful vocabulary to start you off. Look up any words you don't understand in the dictionary. You should listen to how these phrases are pronounced on the audio track.

Time phrases:

- plus tard
- à l'avenir

- quand je serai plus grand(e)/âgé(e)
- après le lycée/après la fac

Future plans:

- Je voudrais être pompier.
- Je voudrais travailler comme vétérinaire.
- Je voudrais travailler dans le domaine du commerce.
- J'aimerais devenir infirmier.
- J'aimerais travailler avec les animaux.
- J'ai envie de travailler dans le tourisme.
- J'ai envie de travailler avec les enfants.

- J'ai l'intention de travailler avec le public.
- Je serai coiffeuse.
- J'irai à la fac pour étudier les sciences.
- Je vais faire une formation professionnelle de mécanicien.
- Je vais faire un apprentissage d'électricien.

 **ACTIVITY** MY IDEAL JOB – MON MÉTIER IDÉAL

Listen to the audio track to hear three people talking about their future plans. Note down as much information as you can about the following:

1. What job do they want to do?

2. Why? (try to name at least four things)

3. What training or qualifications are they going to get?

GRAMMAR

Once you have completed the listening task, read through the transcript online at www.brightredbooks.net/N5French. Is there any vocabulary that you don't know and you need to look up in the dictionary? Have a look at the following phrases taken from the transcript:

 contd

- j'aimerais devenir
- j'irai à la fac
- je pourrai rencontrer
- j'aurai l'occasion de

- je gagnerai
- je serai
- je voudrais être
- ce serait génial

Can you remember what the two tenses above are called? Refer to page 88 to revise the conditional, which tells you what someone *would do*, and refer to page 29 to revise the simple future tense, which tells you what someone *will do*.

⚙ ACTIVITY: MY FUTURE PLANS – MES PROJETS POUR L'AVENIR

Once you have revised these tenses, complete the following sentences, putting the verb in brackets into the simple future tense. Then translate the sentences into English.

1. Je _____ avec le public, peut-être dans un magasin, parce que j'aime le contact avec d'autres personnes. (travailler)

2. Je _____ cuisinier dans un grand restaurant célèbre. (être)

3. J'ai envie de soigner les malades car ça me _____ l'occasion d'aider différentes personnes. (donner)

4. Je _____ pour une grande entreprise internationale, peut-être dans le secteur d'informatique. (travailler)

5. Je _____ un métier créatif parce que j'adore le dessin. (faire)

6. Je ne sais pas encore ce que je _____ à l'avenir mais je sais que j'_____ à l'étranger. (faire/habiter)

7. Je _____ un métier qui me _____ de voyager autour du monde. (chercher/permettre)

8. Je _____ un diplôme au lycée technique. (faire)

9. Si je réussis à mes examens, j'_____ à la faculté et je _____ mes études. (aller/continuer)

10. Je _____ joueur de basket professionnel et je _____ beaucoup d'argent. (être/gagner)

⚙ ACTIVITY: WHAT WOULD YOU DO? – QU'EST-CE QUE TU FERAIS?

Now try the same activity but change the verbs into the conditional tense.

THINGS TO DO AND THINK ABOUT

Now it's your turn. Write about your future plans and do your best to cover the following bullet points. Use the language in this section to help you but personalise the phrases so they are relevant to you. Don't forget that you can learn this and you may wish to use it for your Performance and your writing in the Course assessment.

- What job do you want to do in the future?
- Where would you like to work/live?
- Why do you think you are suitable for this job?
- Why do you want to do this job?
- What training/qualifications do you need to do this job?

➕ DON'T FORGET

Verbs like *être, avoir, aller* and *faire* all have irregular stems in the simple future tense and the conditional tense. You can use the verb tables in your dictionary to look them up if you can't remember their irregular forms.

VIDEO LINK

Check out the clip 'Professions, languages and nationalities' to hear about a variety of jobs you may be interested in: www.brightredbooks.net/N5French

✔ ONLINE TEST

Take the 'Future plans' test online to see how well you know this topic at www.brightredbooks.net/N5French

CULTURE

HOLIDAYS – LES VACANCES 1

DON'T FORGET

You may also wish to talk about your best holiday/trip as part of your Performance.

VIDEO LINK

The clip 'My favourite holiday' will also give you some extra vocabulary and ideas: www.brightredbooks.net/N5French

REVISION – LA RÉVISION

In this section you will learn how to describe your best holiday/trip and give your opinions on travelling. This section is a great way to revise your past tenses (both perfect and imperfect) – you should refer to pages 43 and 67–9 as well as the vocabulary and phrases you have already learned when revising.

- Où
- Quand
- Avec qui
- Logement
- Les vacances
- Activité
- Opinion
- Pendant combien de temps

Let's start by brainstorming all the vocabulary and phrases you know about holidays.

WHEN – QUAND

You could refer to when your holiday is/was in a number of ways:

- en été/en hiver/en automne/au printemps (dernier)
- a Noël
- l'an dernier/l'année dernière

- le mois dernier
- pendant les (grandes) vacances
- il y a un an

WHERE – OÙ

Remember that in French in order to say 'to' or 'in' a country, we use *en* for feminine countries, *au* for masculine countries and *aux* for plural countries. We use *à* for a city or a town.

Here are some examples:

- en France/Espagne/Allemagne
- au Portugal/Maroc/Canada/Pakistan
- aux États-Unis/Pays-Bas
- à Barcelone/Paris/Londres

- à l'étranger
- au bord de la mer/à la campagne/à la montagne
- dans un village/une grande ville

VIDEO LINK

Watch the two 'Holidays in France' clips to hear about where French people go on holiday in July: www.brightredbooks.net/N5French

ACTIVITY — WITH WHOM – AVEC QUI

You could be going on holiday with a variety of different people. For example:

- avec ma famille/en famille
- avec ma femme

- avec mon ami(e)
- avec mon mari
- avec mes amis

- avec l'école
- tout(e) seul(e)

Remember there are three words for 'my' in French. Try to complete the following grammar rule from memory:

There are three words for 'my' in French. These are _____, _____and _____. We use ma for _____ words, _____ for masculine words and _____for plural words.

 **ACTIVITY:** FOR HOW LONG? –
PENDANT COMBIEN DE TEMPS?

You'll need to consider how long your trip lasted:

- quinze jours
- deux semaines
- huit jours/une semaine
- trois mois

Thinking about the length of your trip, try translating the following sentences:

1. En été dernier, je suis allé(e) à Lyon en France pendant quinze jours avec mes amis.
2. Pendant les grandes vacances, je suis parti(e) en famille au bord de la mer en Espagne.
3. A Noël, j'ai passé deux semaines dans un petit village au Canada avec ma mère.
4. Il y a trois ans, je suis allé(e) tout(e) seul(e) à la montagne, en Suisse, pendant un mois.

Now it's your turn – write a sentence about your best holiday/trip.

 ACTIVITY: ACCOMMODATION – LOGEMENT

Choosing from the list below, write in the facilities you could find in the following places.

Logement – accommodation	Equipements/installations – facilities
Dans un hôtel	
Dans une auberge de jeunesse	
Dans un camping	
Dans un gîte	
Chez la famille	
Chez des amis	

une piscine chauffée   un restaurant   un bar   des courts de tennis

une salle de gym   un jardin   un balcon   une belle vue   une grande cuisine

une piste de danse   une salle de jeux   ma propre chambre

 ONLINE TEST

Test yourself on holidays online at www.brightredbooks.net/N5French

Using this vocabulary, write about the accommodation on your holiday. Start with J'ai logé/On a logé ...

 ACTIVITY: LEISURE ACTIVITIES – ACTIVITÉS DE LOISIRS

Here are a few activities you may do on holiday. Check that you understand the meaning of each phrase. You will have many more ideas so just add them to this list.

aller à la plage/piscine
aller en boîte
aller au cinéma
aller au musée
aller au parc d'attraction
faire de la voile
faire de la planche à voile
faire de la natation
faire du sport
faire du ski

faire de l'équitation
lire un roman
écouter de la musique
visiter les environs
manger au restaurant
acheter des souvenirs
se promener
se baigner
bronzer

 THINGS TO DO AND THINK ABOUT

The activities above are in the infinitive to allow you to change them to the imperfect or perfect tense depending on what you want to say. Try writing five sentences about a holiday you have had and what activities you did there.

HOLIDAYS – LES VACANCES 2

VIDEO LINK

Head to the BrightRED Digital Zone and watch the clip 'L'hôtel Guadeloupe', which will give you some extra vocabulary and ideas.

PAST TENSES REMINDER

Remember:

- The perfect tense is an action that is completed in the past, for example *Un jour on est allé au parc d'attraction.*

- The imperfect tense is used for regular actions in the past/interrupted actions and descriptions, for example *Tous les soirs on allait au restaurant pour y déguster les spécialités de la région.*

- You can, however, leave verbs in the infinitive, for example *Je passais mes journées à + infinitive.*

ADDING INTEREST

To make this section more interesting and not just one long list of activities, you may wish to use the following expressions:

- On passait nos journées à + infinitive

- Quand il pleuvait on/je (+ imperfect) …

- Quand il faisait beau on/je (+ imperfect) …

- Tous les jours on/je (+ imperfect) …

- Un jour on/je (+ perfect) …

- Une fois on/je (+ perfect) …

⚙ ACTIVITY: GRAMMAR/TRANSLATION ACTIVITY – UNE EXERCISE DE GRAMMAIRE/TRADUCTION

Look at the following three paragraphs. Fill in the gaps by translating the verb into French and deciding whether you will use it in the perfect or imperfect tense or leave it in the infinitive. You can then try to translate the three paragraphs.

Veronique

1. L'année dernière en hiver je _____ (*to go*) en France avec mes parents. On _____ (*to spend*) nos journées à _____ (*to ski*) dans les Alpes et puis le soir on _____ (*to go*) au restaurant pour _____(*to eat*) de bons repas chauds. Un jour on _____ (*to go*) dans la ville la plus proche pour _____ (*to buy*) quelques souvenirs pour la famille et les amis.

Olivier

2. Il y a trois ans je _____ (*to leave*) en Espagne avec mes amis. Tous les jours on _____ (*to go*) à la plage ou on _____ (*to stay*) au bord de la piscine pour _____ (*to sunbathe*). On _____ (*to spend*) nos soirées en boite de nuit parce qu'on _____ _____ (*to love to dance*). Un jour on _____ (*to windsurf*).

Rose

3. Pendant les grandes vacances je _____ (*to go*) en Italie avec ma mère. Les jours de soleil on _____ (*to walk*) dans de petits villages, on _____ (*to visit*) les environs ou on _____ (*to drink*) un verre à la terrasse des cafés. Un jour on _____ (*to go*) à Rome pour _____ (*to visit*) les attractions touristiques et pour _____ (*to go shopping*).

VIDEO LINK

Check out the 'Travelling to France' clip at www.brightredbooks.net/N5French for the first instalment of Michael's video diary about planning a holiday in France.

 **ACTIVITY:** OPINION OF THE TRIP –
OPINION SUR LE VOYAGE

You will always have an opinion of your trip. Decide if the following expressions are positive or negative and put them under the heading *positive* or *negative.*

C'était super   Le personnel était très serviable   Je me suis bien amusé(e)

C'était intéressant   Je n'y retournerai pas   Les gens étaient très impolis

C'était amusant   Il pleuvait tous les jours   C'était ennuyeux

Je recommanderais ce genre de voyage   Il n'y avait rien à faire

Les gens étaient très accueillants   Les gens n'étaient pas gentils

La nourriture était délicieuse   C'était nul!   C'était sale

La nourriture n'était pas très bonne   Les gens étaient très aimables

 **ACTIVITY:** THE IMPORTANCE OF TRAVEL –
L'IMPORTANCE DE VOYAGER

You could also add why you think travel is important.

In groups try to think, in French, of ways of saying you like to travel and reasons why.

Listen to the audio track and match the parts of the sentences:

 VIDEO LINK

Watch the 'Staying in a castle' clip at www. brightredbooks.net/N5French for more vocabulary.

Saying you love to travel	Reasons
J'adore voyager parce que/car ...	... on découvre de nouvelles cultures et traditions.
J'aime aller à l'étranger parce que/car ...	... voir comment vivent d'autres personnes.
J'aime partir en vacances parce que/car ...	... on se fait de nouveaux amis.
J'aime visiter des pays étrangers parce que/car ...	... de découvrir d'autres pays et d'apprendre une autre langue.
Il est important de voyager pour ...	... on se détend et on oublie la vie quotidienne.
A mon avis voyager est un bon moyen ...	... on profite du beau temps.

Now try to translate them into English.

 ACTIVITY: CÉDRIC'S BEST HOLIDAY –
LES MEILLEURES VACANCES DE CÉDRIC

Before you try to write about your best holiday, listen to Cédric talking about his best holiday. Complete the table by putting in as much information as you can.

Quand – when	
Où – where	
Avec qui – with whom	
Pendant combien de temps – for how long	
Logement – accommodation	
Activité – activities	
Opinion – opinion	

 DON'T FORGET

When writing about a past event make sure you:
- use the perfect and imperfect correctly
- agree the past participles for feminine and plural
- add some opinions
- always check your written accuracy.

 ONLINE TEST

Test yourself on holidays online at www. brightredbooks.net/N5French.

THINGS TO DO AND THINK ABOUT

Now it's your turn. Using all the phrases and passages above to help you, write about a past holiday you have been on.

EVENTS, LITERATURE AND FILM – LES TRADITIONS, LA LITTÉRATURE ET LES FILMS 1

ONLINE

Head to the BrightRED Digital Zone and follow the 'Culture in Montreal', 'Senegal profile' and 'Culture in the Seychelles' links to some websites you may find useful.

VIDEO LINK

Have a look at the BBC clips on special events: 'Family and marriage' and 'Family celebrations' at www. brightredbooks.net/N5French

CELEBRATING A SPECIAL EVENT – CÉLÉBRATION D'UN ÉVÉNEMENT SPÉCIAL

As part of the National 5 course you will be discovering new things about different traditions, special events and cultures in the countries in which French is spoken. It would be impossible to cover every eventuality in this book.

This may be the perfect opportunity for you to do some individual research on an aspect of the culture of a Francophone country. You could present your findings as part of your Performance.

Here are some traditions and cultural events that you may wish to find out more about:

ACTIVITY: TRADITIONS AND SPECIAL EVENTS – LES TRADITIONS ET ÉVÉNEMENTS SPÉCIAUX

Here is some vocabulary you may wish to use when talking about traditions and special events. Try to work out what the words mean in English.

Verb	English
fêter	
manger	
boire	
danser	
chanter	
se déguiser	
prier	

Noun	English
une fête	
des cadeaux	
un gâteau	
les feux d'artifice	
du champagne	
un déguisement	

Use the words above to describe a special event or tradition in Scotland.

LITERATURE AND FILM – LA LITTÉRATURE ET LES FILMS

In this section you will learn how to talk about any books you have read or films you have seen. The language used to describe books and films is very similar so we will look at both together.

Let's start by thinking about what you might like to say about a book or a film:

- What is the book/film about?
- Who are your favourite characters/actors?
- What is your opinion of the book/film?

 **ACTIVITY** WHAT IS THE BOOK/FILM ABOUT? – DE QUOI PARLE LE FILM/LE LIVRE?

Read the sentences/phrases below and translate them into English. You may wish to change or complete them to talk about a book you have just read or a film you have seen.

Le livre/le film se passe au 20ième siècle et a lieu dans le sud de la France.

Le livre/le film parle de …

Le livre/le film raconte l'histoire de …

 ONLINE TEST

Test yourself on events, literature and film online at www.brightredbooks.net/N5French

 **ACTIVITY** YOUR FAVOURITE CHARACTERS – TES PERSONNAGES PRÉFÉRÉS

Here are some adjectives which can be used to describe characters (refer back to pages 8–9 in the Family and friends section for more examples).

Write out the feminine versions and English translations of these adjectives. Then use some of the adjectives to describe your favourite characters/actors.

Masculine	Feminine	English
beau		
marrant		
méchant		
crédible		
ennuyeux		
jeune		
vieux		

Mon personnage/acteur préféré était/est
_____ car il/elle est + *adjective*

Je trouve les personnages/acteurs très crédibles ce qui rend le livre/le film plus intéressant.

Les personnages du livre/du film sont/étaient intéressants car …

Selon moi/à mon avis/je trouve que le scénario est très intéressant et j'ai bien aimé la relation entre les personnages.

 **ACTIVITY** YOUR OPINIONS – TON OPINION

Look at these opinions about a book/film and decide if they are positive or negative, then translate them into English.

Ce que j'ai vraiment aimé c'est …

J'ai vraiment aimé le livre/le film car …

Je trouvais le film un peu long mais j'ai vraiment aimé les acteurs et l'histoire.

Je n'avais jamais lu/vu ce genre de livre/de film mais je le recommanderais car l'histoire est vraiment intéressante.

Je n'ai pas aimé ce livre/ce film car l'histoire était très ennuyeuse.

J'ai été déçu par la fin du livre/du film.

J'ai beaucoup appris/découvert sur la culture française par exemple, les français attachent beaucoup d'importance à passer du temps en famille autour d'un bon repas.

Normalement, je ne regarde jamais les films scientifiques/d'amour/d'action mais ce film m'a beaucoup plu.

J'ai vraiment aimé ce film et je regarderai bien d'autres films de ce genre à l'avenir.

Je recommanderais ce livre/ce film parce que l'histoire m'a beaucoup intéressée et j'aime beaucoup les acteurs.

Je ne recommanderais pas ce livre/ce film car il n'était pas intéressant et il ne se passe rien.

Je n'ai pas aimé ce film car je n'aime pas les films d'action trop violents.

 THINGS TO DO AND THINK ABOUT

Take some of the sentences from the activities above and write a short paragraph about your favourite book/film.

EVENTS, LITERATURE AND FILM – LES TRADITIONS, LA LITTÉRATURE ET LES FILMS 2

VIDEO LINK

You may also wish to watch the BBC clip 'My favourite films and directors' at www.brightredbooks.net/N5French to enhance your vocabulary.

ACTIVITY OPINIONS ON A FILM – AVIS SUR UN FILM

Read the following text, in which Yannick describes a film he has just seen. Answer the questions that follow.

Yannick donne son avis d'un film qu'il vient de voir

La semaine dernière, je suis allé au cinéma pour voir un film britannique. Le film était en anglais et a lieu dans un petit village dans le sud de l'Angleterre. Le film raconte l'histoire de quatre amis qui ne se sont pas vus depuis 15 ans et qui se retrouvent pour un week-end dans une petite maison. Au début les personnages s'entendent très bien et se rappellent de bons moments de leur jeunesse. Mais au cours du film, il commence à y avoir de la tension entre eux. A la fin du film ils se rendent compte que leur vie a changé et qu'ils n'ont plus rien en commun. Mon personnage préféré est Louisa, car elle est très bonne actrice et très crédible dans le rôle.

Le film était assez intéressant et les acteurs jouaient bien. C'était bien de voir un film sous-titré pour pouvoir améliorer mon anglais.

1. When did Yannick see the film? (1)

2. Where does the film take place? (1)

3. What is the film about? (1)

4. What happens:
   (a) at the beginning of the film? (1)
   (b) during the film? (1)
   (c) at the end of the film? (2)

5. Why is Louisa Yannick's favourite character? Mention **two** things. (2)

6. What is Yannick's overall impression of the film? Tick the correct box. (1)

Yannick thought the film was uninteresting and boring.	
Yannick thinks French films are better and the actors were good.	
Yannick likes watching films with subtitles as they help to improve his English.	

Now it's your turn. Write about a film you have seen using the vocabulary and expressions you have learned. Again you may wish to use some of this for your performance.

ACTIVITY: SYLVIE'S OPINION ON A BOOK – L'AVIS DE SYLVIE SUR UN LIVRE

Now listen to Sylvie talking about a book she has just read. Complete the text below by choosing the correct word from the box for each gap.

Sylvie parle d'un livre qu'elle vient de lire

Je viens de lire un livre très (1)_____. Le livre a lieu en (2)_____ et c'est une histoire vraie qui raconte l'expérience un couple de (3)_____ britannique qui déménage dans un petit village en France. Au (4)_____ ils trouvent la vie un peu difficile car ils ne (5)_____ pas la langue et la grande ville leur manque. Mais au bout de quelques (6)_____ ils font la connaissance de villageois et (7)_____ à mieux parler français. Mon personnage (8)_____ est Paul, l'homme du couple. Il est très (9)_____ et optimiste que tout allait bien se passer. A la fin du livre il adore vivre dans ce petit village et il apprécie (10)_____ la culture et la bonne cuisine (11)_____. J'ai vraiment aimé ce livre et je le recommanderais car il est à la fois émouvant et (12)_____.

1. intéressant/intéressante	2. 2004/2005
3. retraités/retraitées	4. debout/début
5. parlent/parle	6. moi/mois
7. commence/commencent	8. préféré/préférée
9. marrante/marrant	10. beacoup/beaucoup
11. français/française	12. drôle/drôlée

 ONLINE TEST

Test yourself on events, literature and film online at www.brightredbooks.net/N5French.

THINGS TO DO AND THINK ABOUT

Now you have all the vocabulary and phrases you need to describe literature and film, you may wish to start reading and/or watching films in French. This is great way to improve your language skills and also gives you an insight into the culture of Francophone countries.

Write about a book you have read using the vocabulary and expressions you have learned. You may wish to use some of this for your Performance.

COURSE ASSESSMENT

OVERVIEW

The Course assessment at National 5 will take the form of an Assignment (writing assignment), a Performance (talking assessment) and two question papers allowing you to demonstrate your reading, writing and listening skills in French.

COMPONENT 4: ASSIGNMENT – WRITING

You will be asked to produce a piece of wriing of 120–200 words in the Modern Language using detailed language based on one of the following contexts: society, learning or culture. The context of employability will be assessed in question paper 1. Throughout the year, you will prepare written pieces of work based on the topics studied which will help you to prepare for the assignment – writing.

The assignment – writing is:

- Set by your centre within SQA guidelines
- Conducted under a high degree of supervision and control in the classroom
- Externally marked by SQA

The assignment – writing has a total allocation of 20 marks, which is scaled to 15 marks.

COMPONENT 5: PERFORMANCE – TALKING

You will be assessed on at least two of these four contexts: society, learning, employability, and culture.

The Performance will allow you to demonstrate your ability to communicate orally in French. After studying the topics at National 5, you will have prepared written pieces of work that should help you with your Performance. The Performance is made up of two parts:

- presentation – 10 marks
- conversation – 20 marks

Presentation

You will be required to give a spoken presentation in French, using detailed language on a topic chosen from one of the following contexts:

- society
- learning
- employability
- culture.

You will choose the topic and develop it into a short presentation of approximately 1–2 minutes to allow demonstration of your language skills, accuracy, pronunciation and intonation.

You will be allowed to refer to up to five headings of no more than eight words each as prompts during the presentation and/or use visual aids. The headings may be in French or English.

You teacher/lecturer will listen to your presentation and ask questions based on it in order to engage you in a conversation on the topic.

contd

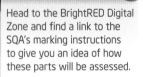

ONLINE

Head to the BrightRED Digital Zone and find a link to the SQA's marking instructions to give you an idea of how these parts will be assessed.

Conversation

Following the prepared presentation and any follow-on questions, you will be required to take part in a conversation using detailed language on a different topic and context and to respond to some questions on that topic. The information to be exchanged will be mainly of a factual nature, but should also include some ideas and opinions. You may also ask questions where appropriate during the conversation.

Within this section marks will be awarded as follows:

- 15 marks for conversation
- 5 marks for the ability to sustain the conversation.

TOP TIPS FOR TACKLING THE EXAM

- If possible, do some practice exam papers beforehand.
- Ensure you go to bed early the night before, having done all of your revision well in advance. If you are tired on the day it will affect your Performance.
- Ensure that your mobile phone is switched off and not kept in your pocket. If your phone goes off during the Course assessment you could be asked to leave the room.
- Make sure you check that you have the right paper in front of you as soon as you sit down. Usually you will be given the correct one but mistakes can be made so don't risk it!
- Read the introduction carefully and use the questions to help lead you to the answer.
- Only use the dictionary if absolutely necessary. The first word you see in the dictionary may not be the one you need so do read all meanings and choose the one that makes the most sense.
- Use *all* the time given and check your answers carefully. Remember, if they do not make sense to you, they will not make sense to the marker. *Check your English too!*

HOW DOES THE SQA ARRIVE AT YOUR FINAL GRADE?

Once you have competed all of your external assessments, each of the scaled marks you achieve will be added together and the examiners will give you an overall mark out of 100 which will translate into your grade. The percentages for achieving each grade vary, but obviously the higher the better!

THINGS TO DO AND THINK ABOUT

Now you should know:

- what is meant by the term 'Course assessment'
- what is involved in your Performance
- what is involved in the Reading/Writing paper
- what is involved in the Listening paper
- what is involved in the assignment – writing

Be sure to make good use of this book and all of your course materials while you prepare for your National 5 assessments – you have the skills and the tools necessary to succeed and as long as you do your best you will achieve a grade of which you can be proud. Stay relaxed and focused and, most of all, bonne chance!

WRITING

INTRODUCTION AND BULLET POINT 1

The aim of this section is to ensure you feel fully prepared for the Writing section of the Course assessment.

You will be revising some of the vocabulary and grammatical structures you have already visited in this book and will build on these to allow you to produce an accurate piece of writing that you feel comfortable with and are able to reproduce and adapt slightly on the day of your Course assessment.

The writing part of the Course assessment is worth a total of 20 marks (scaled to 15 marks) and will be 120–200 words in length. You may wish to write more, but remember that accuracy is key.

So let's begin!

WHAT IS EXPECTED?

First of all, let's look at what you will be expected to write.

You will be expected to write an email in response to a job advert. The job advert will be in French, advertising the job and giving other relevant details, such as the type of person you must be and whom to contact.

You will then have to write your email based on the four predictable bullet points (these will always be the same) and the two less predictable bullet points (these will change from year to year, but will always be in the context of applying for the job).

Below is an example of the job advert and the bullet points you will to have to address. The first four bullet points are the predictable ones and the remaining two the less predictable ones.

You are preparing an application for the job advertised below and you write an email in French to the company.

> **Café Georges** au centre de Bruxelles cherche **serveur/serveuse**.
>
> Vous devez être motivé et dynamique et savoir parler le français et l'anglais.
>
> Pour plus de détails ou si ce poste vous intéresse contactez Mme Georges à l'adresse suivante cafegeorges@fsnet.fr.com.
>
> Veuillez joindre votre CV et répondre par email, incluant les détails suivants.

To help you to write your email, you have been given the following checklist of information to give about yourself. You must deal with all of these points:

- personal details (name, age, where you live)
- school/college education experience until now
- skills/interests you have which make you right for the job
- related work experience
- when you will be available for interview and to work
- any links to Belgium or another French-speaking country.

Use all of the above to help you write the email in French, which should be 120–200 words. You may use a French dictionary.

As you will be talking about yourself in this email it is important to go back and revise present tense verbs, especially the **big four** (avoir, etre, aller, faire) and endings (refer to page 7).

We will take each bullet point in turn.

BULLET POINT 1: PERSONAL DETAILS (NAME, AGE, WHERE YOU LIVE)

This should be a very straightforward start as you will have seen and used these phrases in many other contexts. However you must know how to *spell* these sentences.

Test yourself: Choose the correct phrase from the following.

Name

Je m'applle ...	Je ma pelle ...	Je m'appelle ...
Mon famille nom est ...	Mon nom de famille est ...	Mon surnom est ...

Age

Je suis 16 ans	J'ai 16	J'ai 16 ans
Mon anniversaire est le 12 mai	Mon anniversary le 26 octobre	Mon anniversaire est le 4th juin

Where you live

J'habeet ...	J'habite ...	Je habite ...
à Ayr en Eccosse	à Glagow a Ecossais	à Inverness en Ecosse

How did you do? It is really important that you get off to a good start and ensure your basic French is accurate.

This first bullet point does not allow for a lot of extra French, although you may wish to write more about where you live. (Refer back to the section on town compared to country in the Society chapter (pages 40–1) for a recap of relevant vocabulary.)

Look at the following examples and translate them into English.

Some words have been underlined so that you can adapt the passage to suit your needs.

> **EXAMPLE**
>
> Bonjour, je m'appelle Thomas et j'ai 16 ans. Mon anniversaire est le 16 octobre et j'aurai 17 ans. J'habite à Thurso dans le nord-est de l'Ecosse. Thurso est une petite ville au bord de la mer et il y a environ 10 000 habitants.

> **EXAMPLE**
>
> Je m'appelle Julie et mon nom de famille est Brown. J'ai 15 ans mais j'aurai 16 ans dans deux semaines. J'habite dans un petit village à la campagne qui se trouve à 20 minutes de Glasgow et à 30 minutes d'Edimbourg, qui est la capitale de l'Ecosse.

> **EXAMPLE**
>
> Bonjour, je m'appelle Christina et j'aurai 19 ans le 12 septembre. En ce moment j'habite à Perth qui se trouve au centre de l'Ecosse mais je suis d'origine polonaise. J'habite en Ecosse depuis 10 ans et j'aime bien ce pays car le paysage est magnifique.

> **EXAMPLE**
>
> Je m'appelle John Mackay et j'ai 17 ans. Je vis à Glasgow en Ecosse dans un quartier qui s'appelle Mosspark. J'aime bien mon quartier car il y a beaucoup à faire et tous mes amis y habitent.

 DON'T FORGET

If you are struggling with some of the words, speak to your teacher/lecturer to see if you could make any changes.

 VIDEO LINK

Watch the clip 'J'habite à Dijon' at www. brightredbooks.net/N5French

 VIDEO LINK

Watch the clip 'How to introduce yourself' at www. brightredbooks.net/N5French

ONLINE TEST

Take the 'Writing: Introduction and personal details' test online at www. brightredbooks.net/N5French

Top tips

- Always write sentences that *you* feel comfortable with and that you can cope with when you have to write them off by heart.
- Start learning each paragraph as you write it so you can reproduce it accurately on the day.

- Read your paragraph.
- Cover the first sentence and try to write it out.
- Check.
- Repeat the process until you have written the whole paragraph accurately.

 THINGS TO DO AND THINK ABOUT

Now it's your turn. Write a short paragraph on the first bullet point, including:

- your name
- your age
- where you live.

BULLET POINT 2: SCHOOL/COLLEGE EDUCATION EXPERIENCE UNTIL NOW 1

WHAT TO INCLUDE

This bullet point is about your education experience until now. Let us think about what you may wish to include. If you have already studied the Learning context, then you will already be familiar with a lot of the vocabulary and grammatical structures required to complete this bullet point.

Looking at the spider diagram, it makes sense to start with a brief description of the school/college you are attending.

USEFUL PHRASES

Here are some possible phrases you could use:

Je suis élève à …

Cette année, je suis en première et j'apprends six matières.

Je fréquente _____ où je suis en train de préparer mes examens qui auront lieu au mois de mai.

Puisque j'ai des examens cette année je passe tout mon temps à étudier.

Quant à mon école, c'est une grande école/un grand lycée/une petite école/un petit lycée avec environ 800/500 élèves et 80/40 profs.

J'aime bien mon école/lycée parce que les profs sont, en général, très sympas et j'y ai beaucoup d'amis.

VOCABULARY FOR WHICH SUBJECTS YOU STUDIED

Looking at the spider diagram, four of the points mention your subjects, so it is *really* important that you know these and their gender.

Les matières

Les langues étrangères

le français	l'allemand	l'espagnol	l'italien	
l'urdu	le gaélique	le polonais	le russe	le chinois

Les sciences

la physique	la chimie	la biologie

Les matières obligatoires

l'anglais	les maths

D'autres matières

l'histoire	la géographie	les études modernes/la politique	
le dessin	les arts dramatiques	l'EPS/le sport	la musique

SUBJECTS STUDIED LAST YEAR/SUBJECTS BEING STUDIED NOW

To avoid boring the marker and making too many mistakes, try not to list all the subjects you did last year and all the subjects you are doing this year. Here are some ways you could avoid this:

L'année dernière j'ai fait 6 matières y compris + *two subjects* (*do not forget the article*). Cette année j'ai décidé d'étudier + *subjects* (*do not forget the article*) au niveau National 4/ National 5/Higher.

L'an dernier j'ai étudié 8 matières y compris + *three subjects* (*do not forget the article*) mais cette année je n'étudie que + *subjects*. (*do not forget the article*)

L'année dernière j'ai étudié 6 matières y compris + *two subjects* (*do not forget the article*). Cette année je fais + (du/de la/de l'/des) *subjects* au niveau National 4/National 5/Higher.

When using *faire* with subjects you must change the **definite article**, that is *le/la/l'/les*, to the partitive, that is *du/de la/de l'/des*.

SUBJECTS YOU LIKED/DIDN'T LIKE AND WHY/WHY NOT

Again this should already be quite familiar to you, but it is always good to recap so here are some expressions you could use to give your opinions and talk about subjects you like/dislike:

Opinions

Je trouve que ...   Je pense que ...   A mon avis ...   Selon moi ...

Subjects you like/dislike

Love/like	Dislike/hate
J'adore ...	Je déteste ...
J'aime ...	Je n'aime pas ...
Ma matière préférée est ...	La matière dont j'ai horreur ...
Mes matières préférées sont ...	La matière que j'aime le moins ...

VIDEO LINK

Check out the 'Les cours et les devoirs' clip at www.brightredbooks.net/ N5French.

 THINGS TO DO AND THINK ABOUT

Let's look more closely at what we could say about the subjects we like/dislike.

Put the phrases below under the headings *positif* or *négatif.*

Je suis fort(e) en ...   Je suis faible en ...
A mon avis _____ est très utile.   Je trouve _____ très facile.

Je reçois toujours de bonnes notes en ...
Selon moi _____ est trop difficile.

Je reçois toujours de mauvaises notes en ...
J'ai décidé d'étudier _____ car j'en ai besoin pour ma future carrière.

Je pense que le prof est marrant et il ne nous donne pas trop de devoirs.
A mon avis il est très important d'étudier _____ car _____.
Je trouve que le prof est trop strict et il ne nous aide pas quand on a des difficultés.
J'ai choisi _____ parce que c'est une matière qui m'intéresse.

A mon avis _____ est une perte de temps.

BULLET POINT 2: SCHOOL/COLLEGE EDUCATION EXPERIENCE UNTIL NOW 2

VIDEO LINK

Watch the clip 'Qu'est-ce que tu veux faire dans la vie?' at www.brightredbooks.net/N5French

FUTURE ASPIRATIONS

The second bullet point is probably the best place to add what you would like to do in the future.

Quick reminder

To say what you will do or would like to do later on in life, you will have to use the future or conditional tense. Here is a quick reminder:

Future	Conditional
Take the infinitive	Take the infinitive
Add endings	Add endings
ai, as, a, ons, ez, ont (similar to avoir)	*ais, ais, ait, ions, iez, aient* (like imperfect)
Exceptions	*Exceptions*
être – serai	être – serais
avoir –aurai	avoir –aurais
aller – irai	aller – irais
faire – ferai	faire – ferai

DON'T FORGET

Remember there is no article for jobs.

Other exceptions include pouvoir, savoir, devoir and vouloir.

Now let's look at how you can add what you would like to do in the future. It may be worth linking this to the job and/or languages.

Quand je quitterai l'école j'aimerais aller à la fac pour étudier …

A l'avenir j'aimerais être …

Après avoir fini mes études, j'aimerais prendre une année sabbatique et travailler à l'étranger/en France.

Quand je quitterai l'université j'aimerais passer un an au Québec pour améliorer mon français.

Je ne sais pas encore ce que je veux faire après l'école mais un jour j'aimerais vivre à l'étranger.

ONLINE TEST

Take the 'School/college education experience until now' test online at www.brightredbooks.net/N5French.

THINGS TO DO AND THINK ABOUT

You are now ready and armed with all the phrases you need to write your second bullet point. To help you a little more and also to give you some listening practice, try to complete the following passages about school using the words given in the box below. For a bigger challenge, try not to look at the words.

1. En ce moment, je suis en première au Lycée Ampère. Mon école est très _____ et moderne et il y a environ _____ profs et 1000 élèves. J'aime assez bien mon école car j'y ai beaucoup d'_____ et en général je m'_____ très bien avec tous mes profs.

    L'année _____ j'ai fait 8 matières y compris l'anglais, les maths et l'_____. Cette année j'_____ le français, l'_____, l'espagnol et le dessin. J'adore les langues _____ car selon moi il est très important de _____ parler au moins deux langues de nos _____. Par contre, je n'aime pas trop le dessin. Je _____ que le prof est très _____ et nous donne trop de _____.

    Quand je _____ l'école, j'aimerais aller à la fac pour étudier le _____ et l'espagnol. A l'avenir j'aimerais _____ et vivre à l'_____.

entends	amis	allemand	savoir	sévère
cent	dernière	étranger	jours	français
grande	étudie	étrangères	trouve	devoirs
quitterai	travailler	anglais		

2. Je suis _____ au Lycée Jean Macé ou je suis en _____ de préparer mes examens. Mon lycée est assez _____ mais il est très _____. J'ai de bons rapports avec tous mes profs car ils sont _____ prêts à aider.

    L'an _____ j'ai étudié 9 matières y compris, les maths, les sciences et la _____. Cette _____ je fais du français, des maths, de l'anglais, des sciences et de l'_____. Ma matière préférée, c'est les maths. Je trouve cette _____ très facile et je suis très _____ en maths. D'ailleurs j'ai toujours de bonnes _____. Par _____ la matière dont j'ai horreur c'est la biologie. Je trouve ça trop _____ et à mon _____ c'est inutile.

    A l'_____ j'aimerais aller à la fac pour faire des études de _____. Un jour je veux avoir mon _____ cabinet et bien sûr gagner beaucoup d'_____.

train	avenir	élève	matière	dernier
droit	grand	musique	difficile	vieux
notes	histoire	toujours	propre	forte
contre	avis	argent	année	

BULLET POINT 3: SKILLS/INTERESTS YOU HAVE WHICH MAKE YOU RIGHT FOR THE JOB

This bullet point allows you to write about any skills and/or interests you may have which make you the ideal candidate.

VIDEO LINK

Check out the 'Talking about your work' clip at www.brightredbooks.net/N5French

POSSIBLE WAYS OF STARTING

1. Je veux poser ma candidature pour ce poste parce que …
2. Je suis la personne idéale pour ce poste parce que …
3. Je serais le candidat idéal/la candidate idéale parce que …

These phrases could be followed with a number of different adjectives and phrases. Look at the examples below and choose the ones you feel most comfortable with to complete your sentence.

Je suis …

- travailleur(se)
- gentil(le)
- créatif(ve)
- très ponctuel(le)
- toujours poli(e) et aimable
- toujours souriant(e)
- enthousiaste
- sérieux(se)

Personal qualities

- Je parle couramment le français et l'allemand.
- Je crois que je suis quelqu'un à qui on peut faire confiance.
- On peut toujours compter sur moi.

Refer to page 63 for more phrases about qualities for different jobs.

Other reasons

- J'aimerais gagner de l'expérience en travaillant et en vivant à l'étranger.
- J'adore visiter d'autres pays et faire la connaissance de nouvelles personnes.
- J'aimerais améliorer mon français et découvrir une nouvelle culture.
- J'adore les langues vivantes et j'aimerais me perfectionner en français.
- J'apprends le français depuis 5 ans et j'aimerais travailler en France pour perfectionner mon français.

VIDEO LINK

Watch the clip 'Talking about the working day' at www.brightredbooks.net/N5French

SKILLS PHRASES FOR SPECIFIC JOBS

The phrases above are very general and could be used for any job. Below are some more phrases that are suited to specific jobs.

Tourisme

- Je suis attiré(e) par une carrière dans le tourisme.
- J'aime travailler en équipe.
- Je m'entends très bien avec tout le monde.
- J'aime le contact avec les gens/les clients.

Musée

- Je m'intéresse à l'art/à la peinture/à l'histoire.

Animateur/travail avec les enfants

- Je m'entends très bien avec les enfants.
- J'adore les enfants et je fais du babysitting régulièrement.

contd

- J'ai beaucoup d'énergie et d'enthousiasme.

- Plus tard quand je quitterai l'école j'aimerais travailler avec les enfants.

Vignes/ferme/camping

- J'aimerais travailler dehors/en plein air.
- J'aime les animaux.

INTERESTS RELEVANT TO THE JOB

This bullet point also asks you to mention any interests you may have that may make you right for the job. Really think about this: watching TV or spending time talking to your friends on Facebook etc. are probably not the interests most employers are looking for.

Again, as with bullet point 1, you will have a lot of phrases to talk about your interests. Here are just some ideas of how to make your sentences more interesting.

Possible ways of introducing interests

- Pendant mon temps libre j'aime …
- Quand j'ai du temps libre j'aime …
- Pour me détendre je passe mon temps libre à + *infinitive*.
- Je m'intéresse à la/au/à l'/aux …

- Je me passionne pour …
- J'aime bien …
- Mon passe-temps préféré est _____ car …

Sports

- Je suis très sportif(ve) et je fais du jogging tous les jours. A mon avis il est très important de faire de l'exercice physique pour rester en forme.
- Je fais partie d'un club de …

- Le sport joue un rôle très important dans ma vie.
- Quand il fait beau j'adore faire des randonnées à vélo ou me promener.

Musique

- Pour me reposer je passe mon temps à écouter de la musique.
- Je me détends en écoutant de la musique.

- Je joue de la guitare/du piano depuis cinq ans.
- Je suis passionné(e) par la musique.

Autres intérêts

- J'adore le cinéma et surtout les films étrangers.
- Je m'intéresse beaucoup à l'histoire et donc je vais souvent aux musées.
- Je suis très doué(e) en dessin et j'aime beaucoup peindre et dessiner quand j'ai du temps libre.

- J'adore lire et donc la lecture joue un rôle très important dans ma vie.
- Puisque j'ai des examens cette année je passe la plupart de mon temps à faire mes devoirs.

VIDEO LINK

Have a look at the clip 'Working in a ski resort' at www.brightredbooks.net/N5French.

DON'T FORGET

There will be many other phrases you may wish to use, but just remember you are applying for a job so keep it concise and relevant.

VIDEO LINK

For more about the qualities necessary for work watch the video 'The world of work' at www.brightredbooks.net/N5French

ONLINE TEST

Take the 'Skills/interests you have which make you right for the job' test online at www.brightredbooks.net/N5French.

DON'T FORGET

You can revise more hobbies by flicking to the section 'loisirs' (pp 22–5).

THINGS TO DO AND THINK ABOUT

A bit of a challenge now: try to translate the following sentences into French. This is a really difficult skill but use the phrases you have just learned to help you.

1. I would like to apply for the job as I would like to improve my French.
2. I love travelling and this job would allow me to discover a new culture.
3. I am very hard working and I love working in a team.
4. I would be the ideal person for this job as I am polite and I get on very well with everyone.
5. When I leave school I would like to travel and work abroad.
6. In my free-time I love doing sport. I am in a hockey club and I train every weekend.
7. When I have time I love to go for long walks with my dogs. This keeps me fit and I like being in the fresh air.
8. I am very interested in music and at the moment I am learning how to play the flute.
9. I am very passionate about art and I love to spend my time visiting art galleries.
10. When the weather is nice I like to go horse-riding in the countryside.

BULLET POINT 4: RELATED WORK EXPERIENCE

In this section you will be required to write about any related work experience you may have. This could be about your work experience week or a full-time/part-time job you may currently have. Refer to pages 66–7 to revise the topic of work experience.

QUICK REMINDER

Let's start with any work experience you may have done. You will need to use the perfect and imperfect tenses, so here's just a quick reminder. Refer back to pages 43 and 67–9 if you need more practice on these tenses.

Perfect tense

1. Present tense of avoir or être.

2. Past participle – take the infinitive and remove 'er', 'ir' or 're' and add 'é' to 'er' verbs, 'i' to 'ir' verbs and 'u' to 're' verbs.

3. Remember to learn the irregular verbs, especially the big four: avoir, être, aller and faire.

Imperfect tense

1. Take the present tense 'nous' form of any verb, remove the 'ons' and add the following endings: ais, ais, ait, ions, iez, aient.

2. Great news: the only exception is être.

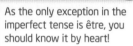

DON'T FORGET

As the only exception in the imperfect tense is être, you should know it by heart!

PAST WORK EXPERIENCE

Now we can start to write about past work experience.

Time phrases

- L'année dernière
- Il y a un an
- Pendant les grandes vacances

Where you worked

J'ai fait un stage/J'ai travaillé …

- dans un restaurant
- dans un supermarché
- dans un bureau

- dans un magasin de vêtements
- dans une bibliothèque
- dans une école primaire

or

DON'T FORGET

You can refer back to the employability section for more jobs.

- J'ai travaillé comme + job (remember no article before the job)

serveur(se)	assistant(e)	femme de chambre
cassier(ère)	vendeur(e)	

ACTIVITY: WHAT YOU DID – CE QUE VOUS AVEZ FAIT

Match the French phrases to the English.

Je devais ...

mettre les tables	look after the children
débarrasser les tables	play with children
classer les dossiers	set the tables
servir les clients	welcome customers
m'occuper des enfants	clear the tables
répondre au téléphone	sort out the files
jouer avec les enfants	serve customers
prendre des commandes	answer the phone
accueillir les clients	take orders

What you thought of it

As you are applying for a job you may wish to make this a positive experience. Here are a few examples of some opinions you could give.

J'ai vraiment aimé ce stage car/parce que ...

- ça m'a donné une première expérience du monde du travail
- j'ai beaucoup appris
- je me suis fait(e) de nouveaux amis en dehors du collège/lycée
- je me suis bien entendu(e) avec tous mes collègues
- c'était intéressant
- j'ai pu gagner mon propre argent

You can mix and match the reasons above, but remember to use the ones you feel most comfortable with and will be able to remember and reproduce accurately.

VIDEO LINK

Check out the clip 'Qu'est-ce que tu veux faire dans la vie?' at www.brightredbooks. net/N5French

ACTIVITY: YANNICK'S WORK EXPERIENCE

Listen to the audio track and answer the following questions.

1. When did Yannick do his work placement? (1)
2. Where did he work? Mention any two things. (2)
3. What tasks did he have to do? (3)
4. Why did he like the placement? Mention any three things. (3)

Now it's your turn. Write a paragraph about any work experience and/or past job you have had.

CURRENT WORK

You may currently have a job and want to write about this. If you have a job at the moment, use the vocabulary you have just learned but change to the present tense. Refer back to page 7 for this. The only real change for this part will be the time phrases:

- En ce moment
- Depuis un an
- Pendant les vacances
- Tous les week-ends/les soirs

You are now ready to write about any job you currently have. Remember this will be in the present tense, but the vocabulary and phrases will remain the same.

ONLINE TEST

Take the 'Related work experience' test online at www.brightredbooks.net/ N5French

THINGS TO DO AND THINK ABOUT

You should now have written the first four predictable bullet points. These bullet points will *always* be part of the job application and if you learn them well you should feel comfortable to reproduce what you have written in accurate French.

BULLET POINTS 5 AND 6: THE UNPREDICTABLE ONES

Now let's move onto the two unpredictable bullet points. These will change every year but will still relate to applying for a job. Don't forget the contexts and topics you will have already covered at National 5, as many of these could help you to complete these unpredictable points.

It would be impossible to try to cover every possibility in this book, but below are a few examples.

We will start with the examples given in the sample question paper at the beginning of this section.

WHEN YOU WILL BE AVAILABLE FOR INTERVIEW AND TO WORK?

- Je serai disponible pour un entretien le 5 juin.
- Je pourrais commencer à travailler chez vous à partir du 1er juillet.

ANY LINKS TO BELGIUM OR ANOTHER FRENCH-SPEAKING COUNTRY?

If you were asked to cover this bullet point you may wish to talk about a past trip to a French-speaking country or maybe you visit a French speaking country on a more regular basis as you have family or friends living there.

Here are a couple of examples to give you an idea of what you could write.

1. Il y a deux ans, je suis allé en Belgique pendant une semaine. J'y suis allé avec en groupe scolaire et on a logé dans une auberge de jeunesse. On a visité beaucoup de monuments et de sites touristiques. Je me suis très bien amusé et j'ai amélioré mon français. J'aimerais bien y retourner.

2. Tous les ans, je passe les grandes vacances en France car ma tante habite un petit village pas loin de Lyon. Je passe les journées à faire des promenades ou à me baigner dans sa piscine. J'adore aller en France. La cuisine française est vraiment délicieuse, il fait souvent très beau et j'aime bien parler en français avec les habitants.

OTHER POSSIBILITIES

You may be required to ask questions about something work related, therefore it is really important you know how to form a question in French so you can adapt your question, no matter what it is.

Question words

What do these question words mean?

- Comment?
- Qui?
- Où?
- Pourquoi?
- Quel/quelle/quels/quelles?
- Que?
- Combien?
- Combien de temps?

To form questions in French you can:

- invert the verb and subject
- use *est-ce que*
- raise your voice at the end of sentence.

ONLINE TEST ✓

Take the 'Unpredictable bullet points' test online at www.brightredbooks.net/N5French.

contd

As this is a written piece, it would be better to use one of the first two possibilities.

Est-ce que je dois porter un uniforme?	or	Dois-je porter un uniforme?
Est-ce que je serai logé(e)/nourri(e)?	or	Serai-je logé(e)/nourri(e)?
Est-ce que je dois travailler les week-ends et les soirs?	or	Dois-je travailler les week-ends et les soirs?
Est-ce que j'aurai des jours de congés?	or	Aurai-je des jours de congés?

Est-ce qu'il y a une navette/des transports en commun de l'aéroport/de la gare jusqu'à chez vous?

or

Y-a-il une navette/des transports en commun de l'aéroport/de la gare jusqu'à chez vous?

There may be other unpredictable bullet points that have not been included here. With your teacher/lecturer you will be able to work on some of your own ideas.

You should now have a complete piece of writing.

TOP TIPS

- Always read the job advert thoroughly and apply for the job that is being advertised.
- Write in paragraphs – this will ensure you cover all the bullet points and make it easier for the marker to check your work.
- Write neatly. Markers have to mark a lot of papers and it is really important that they can read your handwriting.
- The first four bullet points will always be the same, so learn these really well.
- Learn how to spell *Je m'appelle* and remember that in French you use avoir with your age. Get off to good start.
- When talking about where you live, remember to use *à* for a village/town/city and *en* for a feminine country: *en Ecosse, en France.*
- Be careful when talking about your subjects. Make sure you spell them correctly.
- Adjectival agreements – think about these carefully. They need to agree in the feminine singular, masculine plural and feminine plural.
- When writing a date the French say, for example, *le 10 mai.* Do not write *10th mai.*
- When writing about a job, do not use *un* or *une*, for example *En ce moment je travaille comme serveur* not *Je travaille comme un serveur.*
- For the final two bullet points, which are less predictable, make sure your French is accurate. Your teacher/lecturer will have covered many possibilities with you so try to learn these.
- Be careful when asking questions. Either use *Est-ce que* or invert the verb and the subject, for example *Est-ce que je dois travailler le week-end?* or *Dois-je travailler le week-end?*
- Remember to *always* read over your work at the end. Check the following:

  - Does it make sense?
  - Have I covered all the bullet points?
  - Is my spelling accurate?
  - Have I used my accents correctly?
  - Have I agreed adjectives?
  - Are my tenses accurate?

- Finally *only* use the dictionary to check spelling/genders/accents. *Do not* try to translate phrases in your head from English to French.

 ## THINGS TO DO AND THINK ABOUT

Here are some top tips to help you learn:

- Make sure your French is accurate – know your grammar points.
- To help you learn, read a line, close your jotter and write it out again.
- Check over your work.

- Make sure you fully understand what you are writing.
- Change any sentences/phrases you find difficult to remember.
- Only use a dictionary to check spelling. Do not start making up sentences on the day.

- Do not start learning the night before.
- Have a good revision schedule in place.
- Always check your written piece.

LISTENING

UNDERSTANDING LANGUAGE: LISTENING

PREPARING FOR A LISTENING ASSESSMENT

Listening is one of the most challenging skills to master when learning a foreign language. There are lots of ways to prepare for your listening Unit assessments and Course assessment, and this should help to build your confidence before sitting your final exam. Here are some ideas to get you started.

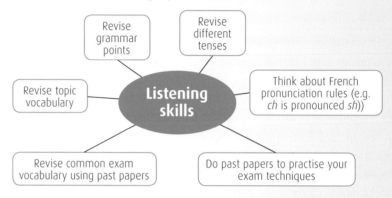

It would be worthwhile revising the following:

- days
- months
- numbers
- time and frequency phrases

- qualifiers and intensifiers (très/vraiment/un peu)
- quantities (trop de/assez de/beaucoup de/peu de)

WHAT IS INVOLVED IN THE LISTENING COURSE ASSESSMENT?

In the Course assessment (the final exam), you will hear a monologue (one person speaking) worth 8 marks and then a dialogue (a conversation between two people on a topic related to the monologue) worth 12 marks. You need to demonstrate your understanding of the text by providing answers in English to the questions asked. The Course assessment in listening will be based on a context that was not covered in question paper 1 (the reading and writing paper). For example, if the reading texts cover society, culture and learning then the listening paper will be on employability. The listening paper is worth a total of 20 marks and there will be 2–3 supported marks, one of which will be in the monologue and will relate to the speaker's 'intent/reason/ attitude/opinion'. You might be aware that this is called the 'overall purpose' question. You will hear the track three times and there will be a break of one minute between each play to let you write your answers.

TACKLING A LISTENING ASSESSMENT

Here are some tips for how to approach a listening comprehension as part of the Unit and Course assessments.

- Start by reading the background information. This will tell you what the text is about.
- Then read the questions carefully.
- The answers usually come in the same order as the questions, so the questions might also give you an idea of what the text is about.

contd

- Pick out key words from the questions and predict key words that you might hear in French. For example, if the question asks what Jean says about his father, you should predict hearing the word 'père'. This will help you to focus on the part of the text that contains the answer.
- Look at the number of marks given for each question so you know how much information to give in your answer.
- When you hear a word you don't understand, imagine how you would spell it. This might help you to identify what it means (think about the pronunciation rules in French).
- Make notes, in French or English, of words that you hear. This could help you when completing your answers because it is challenging to listen and write an answer at the same time. Don't worry about missing information: you will hear the text twice more.
- If you are asked for two things and only manage to catch one in the first hearing, don't panic! Make a mark beside the question and, when you hear the text again, focus on that question and try to add extra information to your answer.
- Once you have heard the text three times, you will have time to check your answers. This is when your notes in English or French could help you.
- Re-read each question and then your answer to make sure you have actually answered the questions.
- Try not to leave any blanks: use your common sense and the key words you have heard to try to put an answer together.

PRACTICE MAKES PERFECT

Remember, by practising listening tasks your techniques, skills and confidence will improve. So let's get started. Listen to the tracks at www.brightredpublishing.co.uk and answer the associated questions over the next few pages. Each listening comprehension will be based on a topic you have already covered in the *BrightRED Study Guide: National 5 French*. Once you have completed the task, mark your answers and ask yourself the following questions.

How could I improve my mark?

- Did I put enough detail in my answers?
- Did my English expression make sense?
- Did I manage to understand tricky vocabulary?
- Did I forget to include key words in my answers (too/really/quite/several)?
- Did I leave out any questions?
- Is there any vocabulary I didn't know?
- Are there any contexts and topic areas I need to revise?

THINGS TO DO AND THINK ABOUT

Record your marks in the table below and monitor your progress.

Self-Evaluation

Topic	Mark in monologue /8	Mark in dialogue /12	Total mark /20
Society: Family and friends			
Society: Leisure and health			
Society: Technology and TV/film			
Society: Home area and the environment			
Learning: Experience at school and future plans			
Employability: Job searches and interviews			
Culture: Holidays			

LISTENING ACTIVITIES 1

SOCIETY

 ACTIVITY 1. FAMILY AND FRIENDS – LA FAMILLE ET LES AMIS

Section 1

Listen to Aurélie talking about her relationships with the members of her family. Answer the following questions.

1. Why does Aurélie say she has a good relationship with her older sister? State any one thing. (1)
2. How does her sister help her? State any one thing. (1)
3. What does she say about her younger brother? State any two things. (2)
4. Aurélie talks about her relationship with her parents.
    (a) What does she say about her father? State any one thing. (1)
    (b) What does she say about her mother? State any two things. (2)
5. What is Aurélie's overall opinion of how she gets on with her family? Tick (√) the correct statement. (1)

She has a very positive relationship with all members of her family.	
She has positive and negative relationships with her family.	
She argues with her parents all the time.	

Section 2

Next, listen to Kevin asking Céline about her friendships. Now answer the following questions.

1. Céline talks about spending time with her friends.
    (a) When does Céline spend time with her friends? State any one thing. (1)
    (b) What does she love doing with them? State any one thing. (1)
2. How does she describe her ideal friend? State any two things. (2)
3. What kind of person would she not like to be friends with? State any two things. (2)
4. She talks about how some young people are influenced by others. Fill in the blanks:

They need to _____ or _____ so they don't feel isolated or excluded. (2)

5. She says that her friends never judge her. State any two examples she gives to support this. (2)
6. She mentions that her sister plays an important role in her life. What does she say? State any two things. (2)

 **ACTIVITY** 2. LEISURE AND HEALTH – LES LOISIRS ET LA SANTÉ

Section 1

Listen to the podcast about Louise's healthy lifestyle and answer the following questions.

1. Her mother prepares the meals at home. What does Louise say about them? State any two things. (2)
2. Louise says she prefers to eat healthily but what are her weaknesses? State any two things. (2)
3. Louise says smoking is stupid. State any two reasons she gives for this. (2)
4. Louise says that a lot of young people drink alcohol. State any one reason she gives. (1)
5. What is Louise's overall opinion of staying healthy? Tick (√) the correct statement. (1)

contd

Staying healthy is a waste of time.	
Leading a healthy lifestyle is important.	
Schools should do more to encourage a healthy lifestyle.	

Section 2

You then listen to Pierre asking Caroline about her free time. Answer the following questions.

1. How often does Caroline train for basketball? State one thing. (1)
2. How does she describe the training? State any two things. (2)
3. Apart from keeping her fit, why does Caroline like playing basketball? State any one thing. (1)
4. Caroline says she likes to spend time with her family.
   (a) Why does she like going shopping with her mother? State any one thing. (1)
   (b) Why does she like going to the cinema with her brother? State any one thing. (1)
5. She doesn't see her father very often.
   (a) Why? State any one thing. (1)
   (b) Which activities do they do together during the holidays? State any one thing. (1)
6. Where did they go on holiday last summer? State two things. (2)
7. Why does she want to go back there? State any two things. (2)

ACTIVITY: 3. TECHNOLOGY AND TV/FILM – LA TECHNOLOGIE, LA TÉLÉ ET LES FILMS

Section 1

You listen to a podcast about technology. Now answer the following questions.

1. Technology has a lot of advantages. State any two examples given. (2)
2. What are the disadvantages of technology? State any two examples given. (2)
3. Young people are really affected by technology. In what way? State any two examples given. (2)
4. What piece of advice is given at the end of the broadcast? (1)
5. What is the speaker's overall opinion about technology? Tick (√) the correct statement. (1)

Overall he thinks technology is a good thing.	
He thinks technology should only be used in the world of work.	
He thinks technology is a waste of time.	

Section 2

Germain talks to Stéphanie about film and television. Listen to the track and then answer the questions below.

1. Why is Stéphanie going to the cinema? (1)
2. Stéphanie talks about thrillers. Why does she like thrillers? State any one thing. (1)
3. Why does she love going to the cinema? Tick (√) the two correct statements. (2)

She loves the atmosphere.	
She loves eating popcorn.	
She loves the lighting in the cinema.	
She loves watching films on a big screen.	

4. She says she doesn't watch television much at the moment. What reasons does she give for this? State any two things. (2)
5. She talks about what she likes to watch on TV.
   (a) Why does she like soap operas? State any one thing. (1)
   (b) Why does she like game shows? State any one thing. (1)
6. What does she like about *Masterchef*? State any two things. (2)
7. She talks about programmes she doesn't like.
   (a) Why doesn't she like sports programmes? State any one thing. (1)
   (b) What annoys her about the adverts? State any one thing. (1)

LISTENING ACTIVITIES 2

SOCIETY

 **ACTIVITY** 4. HOME AREA AND THE ENVIRONMENT – OÙ J'HABITE ET L'ENVIRONNEMENT

Section 1

Listen to Michel talking about his home area. Now answer these questions.

1. How long has Michel lived in this town? (1)
2. His town is 10 minutes from the seaside. What does he like doing there at the weekend? State any one thing. (1)
3. State any two disadvantages he mentions about living in his town. (2)
4. He says he lived in the countryside when he was younger. What did he not like about living there? State any two things. (2)
5. He is moving to Manchester soon. Why is he happy about moving there? State any one thing. (1)
6. What is Michel's overall opinion of living in a big town? Tick (√) the correct statement. (1)

He hates living in a big town.	
He loves living in a big town.	
He would prefer to live in the mountains.	

Section 2

Yannick, a young French man, speaks to Paula about her weekend away at her grandparents' house. Listen to the track and then answer the questions below.

1. Where do Paula's grandparents live? State any one thing. (1)
2. What is their house like? Tick (√) the two correct statements. (2)

They live on a farm.	
There is a big kitchen.	
They have a swimming pool.	
They have a garage.	

3. She says she doesn't get bored at her grandparents'. State any two reasons she gives for this. (2)
4. She talks about what she did at the weekend.
   (a) What did she do on Saturday? State any one thing. (1)
   (b) What did she do on Sunday? State one thing. (1)
5. She says her cousin loves living there. Why does her cousin like living there? State two things. (2)
6. What does her cousin not like about living there? State any one thing. (1)
7. Paula says she loves going to her grandparents' house. State any two reasons she gives. (2)

LEARNING

 **ACTIVITY** 5. EXPERIENCE AT SCHOOL AND FUTURE PLANS – LA VIE SCOLAIRE ET LES PROJETS POUR L'AVENIR

Section 1

Listen to the podcast about Marie's experience at school and then answer the following questions.

1. Why does Marie like her school? State any two things. (2)
2. She talks about the school day. Why does she find it tiring? State any two things. (2)
3. Why is art her favourite subject? State any one thing. (1)
4. What does she say about her art teacher? State any two things. (2)
5. What is Marie's overall opinion of her school? Tick (√) the correct statement. (1)

She likes it but all the teachers are too strict.	
She likes it but the work is too difficult.	
She likes it but she gets too much homework.	

Section 2

Now listen to Jérôme, who asks Sylvie about her future plans. Answer the following questions.

1. Sylvie talks about her plans for the summer holidays.
   (a) What are her plans for the summer holidays? State any one thing. (1)
   (b) Why does she want to do a course in clothes design? State two things. (2)
2. Why will she live at home for the first year of her training? State any one thing. (1)
3. Staying at home doesn't bother Sylvie.
   (a) What does she say about her relationship with her parents? State any two things. (2)
   (b) What is the advantage of living with her mother? State any one thing. (1)

contd

4. Sylvie talks about getting a part-time job.
(a) She would like to work in a _____. (1)
(b) What will she do with the money she earns from her part-time job? State two things. (2)

5. What does she like to do with her friends when they have free time? State any two things. (2)

EMPLOYABILITY

 **ACTIVITY:** 6. JOB SEARCHES AND INTERVIEWS – LA RECHERCHE D'EMPLOI ET LES ENTRETIENS

Section 1

You listen to a radio programme about Olivier, who is looking for a part-time job. Now answer the questions below.
1. Why do Olivier's parents say that he should find a part-time job? State two things. (2)
2. Olivier says he has been looking for a job for five weeks. What jobs are being advertised? State two things. (2)
3. Why is this a problem for Olivier? State any one thing. (1)
4. Last weekend Olivier saw an advert for a job as a tennis coach. Apart from the fact he could play tennis often, why does this job appeal to him? State two things. (2)
5. What is Olivier's overall opinion of finding a job? Tick (√) the correct statement. (1)

It has been quite difficult to find a job.	
You have to go abroad to find a job.	
It has been easy to find a job.	

Section 2

You then listen to Raphaël, who is asking Christine about an interview she is preparing for.
1. How will Christine prepare for her interview? State any two things. (2)
2. What has her mother advised her to wear? Tick (√) the correct statement. (1)

A white skirt.	
A black blouse.	
A black jumper.	

3. Christine gives information about her interview. Where will the interview take place? State any two things. (2)
4. How much will Christine earn if she gets the job? (1)
5. What information does Christine give about the hours of work? State any two things. (2)
6. Christine talks about the ideal person for the job. Which qualities are mentioned? State any two things. (2)
7. Christine mentions the advantages of getting a summer job. State any two things. (2)

CULTURE

 ACTIVITY: 7. HOLIDAYS – LES VACANCES

Section 1

Listen to Hélène talk about her holidays and then answer the questions below.
1. Her aunt lives 15 km from Toulouse in the southwest of France. What does she say about her aunt's house? State any two things. (2)
2. Why does she get on well with Anne, her cousin? State any two things. (2)
3. She says she spends a lot of time with Anne.
   (a) What do they do during the day? State any one thing. (1)
   (b) What do they do if it is too hot? State any one thing. (1)
4. For Hélène, what is the disadvantage of going on holiday? (1)
5. What is Hélène's overall opinion of going on holiday to her aunt's house? Tick (√) the correct statement. (1)

She hates spending her holidays with her family.	
She would prefer to go on holiday with her friends.	
She loves going on holiday to her aunt's.	

Section 2

Laure asks Cédric about his recent holiday to Spain. Listen to the track and answer the following questions.
1. How long did Cédric go to Spain for? (1)
2. Why did he think it was great to go away without his parents? State any two things. (2)
3. He says the holiday started badly. What happened? State any one thing. (1)
4. What does he say about the accommodation? Tick (√) the two correct statements. (2)

They stayed in a youth hostel.	
It was at the seaside.	
There was no bathroom.	
The room was clean.	

5. He talks about what they did on holiday.
   (a) What did they do the first week? State any two things. (2)
   (b) What did they do the second week? State any two things. (2)
6. Apart from the weather, why would he recommend Spain as a holiday destination? State any two things. (2)

APPENDICES

TRANSCRIPTS

WHAT DO YOU LIKE DOING AT SCHOOL? – QU'EST-CE QUE TU AIMES FAIRE AU LYCÉE? (P51)

Frédéric

Cette année je fais six matières. Ma matière préférée, c'est l'espagnol car le prof est patient et compréhensif. J'adore travailler par deux et en groupe parce que je dois communiquer avec mes camarades de classe. Ce que j'aime le plus, c'est parler en espagnol car pour moi, le plus important c'est la communication. Pourtant, je n'aime pas écrire des dissertations car c'est monotone. En plus, apprendre la grammaire peut être difficile.

Corinne

En ce moment, j'étudie cinq matières. Je m'intéresse aux sciences car après le lycée, j'ai l'intention d'étudier la biologie à la fac. Normalement on travaille par deux pour faire des expériences scientifiques, ce que j'adore car c'est vraiment intéressant. Par contre, je n'aime pas passer des heures à faire des recherches sur Internet car ce n'est pas facile de lire et de comprendre beaucoup d'articles scientifiques.

Thierry

Ma passion au lycée, ce sont les maths. J'aime travailler tout seul et résoudre des problèmes d'arithmétique et d'algèbre. Mon prof dit que je suis fort en maths et pour moi, c'est assez facile. Ce que je n'aime pas, c'est passer des examens. Je n'aime pas la pression et je suis toujours nerveux avant les examens.

Anna

Je suis très sportive donc au lycée, ma matière préférée est l'EPS. J'adore faire partie d'une équipe et participer aux jeux sportifs car c'est vraiment amusant et c'est bon pour rester en bonne forme. Je déteste faire les devoirs, comme écrire des dissertations car je les trouve ennuyeuses et je préférerais passer mon temps à faire des activités sportives et physiques.

MÉLANIE'S SCHOOL – L'ECOLE DE MÉLANIE (P57)

Mon lycée se trouve à Charleroi en Belgique. C'est un petit lycée avec cinq cent trente élèves. Je pense que mon lycée est un bon lycée et le bâtiment est petit et moderne. Je vais au lycée en bus scolaire qui est gratuit. Les cours commencent à huit heures vingt et finissent à seize heures quinze. On a six cours par jour et chaque cours dure cinquante-cinq minutes. On n'a pas de cours le mercredi après-midi. Nous avons une récré qui dure vingt minutes et une heure dix pour le déjeuner. La pause du déjeuner est à midi quarante-cinq. Je mange à la cantine avec mes copains et la nourriture n'est pas chère. Malheureusement, il n'y a pas beaucoup de choix et la nourriture n'est pas saine. J'étudie huit matières et ma matière préférée, c'est la musique. Il y a dix-huit élèves dans ma classe. On a de la chance car il y a une grande bibliothèque avec des ordinateurs où nous pouvons faire de la recherche. Je dirais que je n'aime pas mes profs car ils sont très sévères et ils nous donnent trop de devoirs. Il faut porter l'uniforme, ce qui est affreux à mon avis. Tout le monde se ressemble quand on porte l'uniforme. Je préférerais porter des vêtements confortables et à la mode. Ce que j'aime au lycée, c'est qu'il y a des clubs de sport et une chorale après les cours. Ce que je n'aime pas c'est que mes parents doivent acheter les livres et les cahiers pour chacune de mes matières.

 **ACTIVITY:** THE SCHOOL SYSTEM IN SCOTLAND – LE SYSTÈME SCOLAIRE EN ÉCOSSE (P57)

L'année dernière j'ai visité le lycée de mon cousin écossais. Le lycée se trouve à Oban, dans l'ouest de l'Écosse. C'est un grand lycée avec huit cents élèves. Le bâtiment est moderne. Les cours commencent à neuf heures moins dix et ils finissent à quinze heures trente. Il y a une récré à onze heures et la pause déjeuner est à treize heures dix. Normalement, les élèves mangent à la cantine car il y a beaucoup de choix et ce n'est pas cher. De temps en temps, les élèves vont aux magasins pour acheter un sandwich et une boisson. En général les élèves étudient six matières et il y a trente élèves dans chaque classe. Dans son lycée, il faut porter l'uniforme et à mon avis, c'est très chic et très élégant. En ce qui concerne les lycées en Écosse, ce que j'aime le plus c'est que les élèves s'entendent bien avec les profs et il y a beaucoup d'activités parascolaires. En revanche, ce que je n'aime pas, c'est que le règlement est strict, on n'a pas beaucoup de liberté.

ACTIVITY: STUDYING AND WORKING – ÉTUDIER ET TRAVAILLER (P65)

Sophie

Quand j'avais 16 ans mes parents ont décidé de supprimer mon argent de poche et donc, j'étais obligée de trouver un petit boulot. J'ai vu une annonce pour un poste de vendeuse dans la vitrine d'un magasin de vêtements et j'y travaille maintenant tous les samedis.

Au début c'était difficile de gérer mon temps entre le travail et les études. Alors, j'ai dû apprendre à organiser mon emploi du temps—je passe mon dimanche entièrement à étudier et deux heures chaque soir à faire mes devoirs.

J'aime mon travail car ça m'a donné plus de confiance en moi. Je suis devenue plus mûre et en plus, je gagne mon propre argent. Le seul inconvénient est que je suis trop fatiguée pour sortir en semaine.

Christian

Je ne crois pas que les jeunes devraient travailler en même temps qu'étudier. On devrait profiter de sa jeunesse avant de passer sa vie à travailler. Aussi, comme il y a tant de chômeurs, il est injuste de donner un emploi à un étudiant.

À mon avis, il est très important de consacrer du temps à ses études. La réussite aux examens offre plus d'options pour l'avenir. Par exemple, on a plus de chances d'étudier à l'université de son choix, de faire un apprentissage professionnel et de trouver un premier emploi.

À mon avis, il y a d'autres moyens d'acquérir un peu d'expérience de la vie. Moi, par exemple, je fais partie d'une association pour les jeunes du quartier. On organise des randonnées à cheval en campagne, des pièces de théâtre et des fêtes pour les anniversaires. D'accord, je ne suis pas payé, mais en étant membre d'une telle association, j'ai appris à travailler au sein d'une équipe et à communiquer avec des gens de tous milieux.

Céline

Je suis étudiante à la fac à Marseille. Il faut travailler parce que j'ai besoin de gagner de l'argent. J'ai de la chance car mes parents paient le loyer et les frais mais si je veux acheter des vêtements ou sortir avec mes amis, c'est moi qui paie. D'un côté, mon petit boulot me donne de l'indépendance et je peux dépenser mon argent comme je veux. Je ne dépends pas complètement de mes parents. De l'autre côté, je dois travailler vingt heures par semaine, c'est trop à mon avis. Il est difficile de trouver l'équilibre entre les études et mon travail. Souvent je n'ai pas assez de temps de compléter mes devoirs car je dois travailler et par conséquent, mes profs ne sont pas contents.

Pierre

J'étudie l'anglais à l'université à Montréal. Mes parents n'ont pas beaucoup d'argent donc je dois payer le loyer, les frais et les repas. J'ai un petit boulot dans un hôtel comme serveur. Normalement, je travaille le vendredi et le samedi soir. Ce que j'aime le plus c'est que mon travail est bien payé et donc je ne dois pas travailler trop d'heures. Je reçois des pourboires aussi et ça aide ma situation financière. Mes collègues sont amusants et nous sommes amis, ce qui est génial car j'habite loin de mes amis du lycée. Je peux manger ce que je veux au travail et donc je peux économiser de l'argent. Par contre, les heures sont longues et je dois travailler jusqu'à minuit. Par conséquent, je suis souvent fatigué et je trouve qu'il est difficile de se concentrer pendant les cours. Ce que je n'aime pas, c'est que mes amis sortent le weekend et je dois travailler.

APPENDICES

 **ACTIVITY** WHO IS IT? – C'EST QUI? (P70)

Marc

J'ai travaillé dans une école primaire. Le stage m'a offert l'expérience de travailler avec les enfants et l'opportunité d'apprendre comment contrôler les enfants. J'y allais en bus. J'ai travaillé du lundi au vendredi mais je ne travaillais pas le soir.

Stéphanie

Mon stage en entreprise était dans un hôpital. Il fallait porter un uniforme. J'ai appris à soigner les gens malades et j'ai rencontré des gens sympas. J'ai dû préparer le thé et le café. J'allais au travail en train et le trajet prenait vingt minutes. J'ai travaillé le weekend.

Luc

Pendant mon stage en entreprise j'ai travaillé dans un magasin de musique. Il fallait travailler avec le grand public. Le stage m'a donné l'occasion d'apprendre à bien servir les clients et à opérer la caisse. J'ai appris de nouvelles choses et c'était utile.

 **ACTIVITY** MY IDEAL JOB – MON MÉTIER IDÉAL (P72)

A. Le domaine du tourisme m'intéresse beaucoup donc j'aimerais devenir guide touristique. Au lycée, je suis fort en langues étrangères et je pense qu'il est utile de pouvoir communiquer avec les gens de différents pays. À mon avis, j'ai les qualités personnelles pour ce travail. Je suis sociable, poli et j'aime travailler en équipe. À mon avis, c'est un travail de rêve car je pourrai rencontrer beaucoup de nouvelles personnes et peut-être j'aurai l'occasion de voyager à l'étranger avec des groupes de touristes. Après mes examens j'irai dans un lycée technique pour étudier le tourisme.

B. Après avoir quitté le lycée, j'ai envie de devenir médecin. J'ai toujours de bonnes notes en sciences. En ce qui concerne mon caractère, on dit que je suis sympa, serviable et compréhensif. À mon avis, c'est le métier idéal car je pourrai soigner les gens malades et ce serait un travail varié et intéressant. En plus je gagnerai beaucoup d'argent. J'ai l'intention de continuer mes études à la fac pour obtenir un diplôme en médecine.

C. Quand je serai plus grande, je voudrais être professeur de sport. Mon rêve, c'est de travailler en plein air avec les jeunes. Je n'ai pas envie de passer mon temps derrière un ordinateur, je préfère être dehors. Le tennis, c'est ma passion et l'EPS, c'est ma matière préférée au lycée. Je suis capable de faire ce boulot car je suis patiente, énergique et dynamique. Je pense que ce serait génial car je toucherai un bon salaire et j'aurai de longues vacances. J'irai à la fac pour étudier l'enseignement.

 **ACTIVITY** CÉDRIC'S BEST HOLIDAY – LES MEILLEURES VACANCES DE CÉDRIC (P77)

Bonjour, je m'appelle Cédric. En avril dernier je suis allé au Maroc avec des amis. On a pris l'avion et on y a passé huit jours. On a logé dans un hôtel de luxe au bord de la mer. L'hôtel était vraiment beau et il y avait deux grandes piscines, une salle de gym, trois restaurants et deux bars. Nos chambres étaient très grandes et avaient un balcon avec vue sur la mer. Comme il faisait très beau et chaud on passait nos journées à se baigner dans la piscine et à bronzer. Tous les après-midis on se promenait au bord de l'eau et on buvait un thé à la menthe à la terrasse des cafés. Un jour on est allé dans le « souk » qui est un grand marché et là on a acheté des pâtisseries marocaines et quelques cadeaux pour nos amis et familles en France. Un soir on a mangé dans un restaurant typique et on a vu un spectacle avec des femmes qui faisaient la danse du ventre. C'était bien amusant. Je me suis vraiment amusé pendant ces vacances. Les gens étaient très accueillants et en plus ils parlaient le français. À mon avis il est très important de voyager à l'étranger car on découvre de nouvelles cultures, on voit comment les autres gens vivent et bien sûr les vacances sont toujours bonnes pour se détendre.

ACTIVITY: YANNICK'S WORK EXPERIENCE (P93)

Bonjour, je m'appelle Yannick. L'an dernier pendant les vacances de Pâques j'ai fait un stage dans un hôtel au centre de Toulouse. J'ai travaillé comme serveur dans un des restaurants. Je commençais à 11 heures tous les jours et je devais mettre les tables, accueillir les clients et prendre les commandes des clients. J'ai vraiment aimé mon stage car tous les clients étaient sympas et m'ont laissé de bons pourboires. De plus, je me suis bien entendu avec tout le monde et j'ai beaucoup appris à propos de la restauration.

COURSE ASSESSMENT: LISTENING

ACTIVITY: 1. FAMILY AND FRIENDS – LA FAMILLE ET LES AMIS (P98)

Section 1

Je pense qu'il y a des hauts et des bas dans toutes les familles. À mon avis, je m'entends bien avec ma famille, mais il faut dire qu'on se dispute souvent. J'ai une bonne relation avec ma sœur aînée car elle est vraiment compréhensive et toujours disponible pour m'aider. Elle a deux ans de plus que moi, donc elle m'aide à faire mes devoirs et elle m'aide aussi quand j'ai des problèmes avec mes amis.

En ce qui concerne mon frère cadet, je dirais qu'il est énervant car il se moque de moi devant mes amis. Le pire, c'est qu'il utilise mon ordinateur sans demander la permission – il est casse-pieds!

Quant à mes parents, mon père est trop protecteur et il ne me laisse pas sortir avec mes amis pendant la semaine. Je trouve ça injuste.

Avec ma mère, c'est très différent. Elle est respectueuse de ma vie privée. Ce que j'aime le plus, c'est qu'elle me donne assez de liberté et qui on passe beaucoup de temps ensemble.

Section 2

```
Kevin:  Bonjour, Céline. Ça va?

Céline: Oui. Ça va, merci.

K:      Est-ce que tu passes beaucoup de temps avec tes amis?

C:      Je dirais que oui. On passe du temps ensemble le vendredi soir et pendant
        les vacances. Ce que j'adore, c'est inviter mes amis pour regarder un film et
        manger des pizzas ensemble. On rigole et on s'amuse.

K:      À ton avis, qu'est-ce que c'est un ami idéal?

C:      C'est une bonne question. Pour ma part, un bon ami est quelqu'un qui me
        comprend, qui partage mes centres d'intérêts et à qui je peux me confier.

K:      Et quels seraient les traits de caractère d'un mauvais ami?

C:      Personnellement, je ne pourrais pas être amie avec quelqu'un qui me critique
        ou quelqu'un qui est toujours de mauvaise humeur. De plus, je n'aime vraiment
        pas les gens égoïstes.

K:      Quelquefois est-ce que tu te disputes avec tes amis?

C:      Pas vraiment. On s'entend à merveille la plupart du temps.

K:      Tu penses qu'il y a des jeunes qui sont influencés par leurs amis?

C:      Oui, bien sûr. Je connais des jeunes qui sont plus influençables que
        d'autres. Il y en a qui se soucient trop de l'opinion des autres. Par
        exemple, ils croient qu'ils doivent fumer ou boire de l'alcool pour ne pas se
        sentir isolé ou exclu. Je trouve ça triste.

K:      Et toi, tu n'es pas influencée par tes amis?

C:      J'ai de la chance car mes amis ne me jugent jamais. Par exemple, je peux
        porter ce que je veux, aimer des films différents de ceux qu'ils aiment, et
        avoir ma propre opinion.

K:      Alors, qui joue un rôle important dans ta vie et qui t'influence?

C:      C'est ma sœur aînée qui joue le rôle le plus important dans ma vie. Je peux
        parler de tout avec elle, elle est vraiment patiente et elle me donne de bons
        conseils. D'ailleurs, je dois voir ma sœur dans dix minutes. Il faut que je
        me dépêche. À tout à l'heure!

K:      Pas de problème. À bientôt.
```

 **ACTIVITY** 2. LEISURE AND HEALTH – LES LOISIRS ET LA SANTÉ (PP99–100)

Section 1

On dit toujours qu'il est très important de faire attention à sa santé.

Chez nous, c'est ma mère qui prépare les repas. Elle est très bonne cuisinière alors les repas sont toujours délicieux et équilibrés. D'ailleurs ma mère insiste pour qu'ils contiennent toujours des légumes. Personnellement, je préfère manger sainement mais j'ai une faiblesse pour les chips, les bonbons et les gâteaux. Je sais que je ne devrais pas manger trop de matières grasses et sucrées mais ça fait du bien de temps en temps. Ha ha!

À part bien manger, pour rester en bonne santé, il faut aussi éviter de fumer ou de boire trop d'alcool. À mon avis, fumer des cigarettes est vraiment bête. Le tabac coûte cher, l'odeur est dégoûtante et c'est très dangereux pour les poumons!

De nos jours, il y a beaucoup de jeunes qui consomment de l'alcool. Ils pensent que l'alcool aide à se détendre et à devenir plus sociable. J'ai été tentée une fois mais j'avais peur que mes parents soient en colère contre moi.

Section 2

Pierre: Bonjour, Caroline. Ça va?

Caroline: Oui. Ça va bien, merci.

P: Est-ce que tu fais de l'exercice?

C: Oui, j'adore faire du sport. Ce que j'aime le plus, c'est jouer au basket. Je vais à l'entraînement trois fois par semaine et on a des matchs le samedi matin.

P: Ah, bon? C'est beaucoup, non?

C: Je pense que oui. Il faut dire que l'entraînement est fatigant car on doit beaucoup courir! Après les matchs, j'ai toujours envie de dormir. Ha Ha!

P: Alors, pourquoi aimes-tu le basket?

C: Pour ma part, le basket me maintient en bonne forme. Le basket me donne aussi l'occasion de me faire de nouveaux amis en dehors de l'école et de m'amuser.

P: Ah, c'est super. Est-ce que tu as d'autres passe-temps?

C: Oui, bien sûr. J'adore passer du temps avec ma famille. Ce que j'aime le plus, c'est faire les magasins avec ma mère. Elle est très généreuse et elle m'achète toujours un vêtement. J'adore aller au cinéma avec mon frère car on aime les films d'horreur et il me paie un hamburger.

P: Et ton père, est-ce que tu fais des activités avec ton père?

C: Pas vraiment. Je ne vois pas beaucoup mon père car il doit souvent voyager à l'étranger pour son travail. Pourtant, pendant les vacances, nous adorons faire des sports nautiques ensemble, de la planche à voile par exemple. Je trouve cela passionnant et vraiment amusant.

P: Où est-ce que vous passez les vacances?

C: Ça dépend mais, par exemple, l'été dernier nous avons passé deux semaines au bord de la mer dans l'ouest du Maroc. On s'est bien amusés.

P: Tu vas y retourner cet été?

C: Oui, absolument! Les Marocains sont très accueillants, la plupart des Marocains parlent le français et il fait toujours très beau au Maroc. Tu devrais y aller un de ces jours.

P: Ah, oui. Peut-être. Alors, bonnes vacances! Au revoir.

 **ACTIVITY:** 3. TECHNOLOGY AND TV/FILM – LA TECHNOLOGIE, LA TÉLÉ ET LES FILMS (P99)

Section 1

La Technologie

Bonsoir à tous. Ce soir on va parler de la technologie. La technologie joue un rôle très important de nos jours, que ce soit dans le monde du travail, à l'école ou tout simplement dans la vie quotidienne.

Et, effectivement, la technologie a beaucoup d'avantages. Par exemple, grâce à l'ordinateur, on peut rester en contact avec sa famille et ses amis n'importe où. On peut aussi faire des achats en ligne et on peut télécharger des films et de la musique pour pas cher.

Par contre, la technologie a aussi ses inconvénients. Il faut faire très attention lorsqu'on tchate en ligne, les informations personnelles peuvent être volées et ça donne mal à la tête si on reste connecté trop longtemps. Mais ce sont les jeunes qui sont les plus vulnérables aux dangers de la technologie. Par exemple, trop de jeunes ne peuvent plus se passer de leur téléphone portable et, par conséquent, ils passent beaucoup moins de temps à lire ou à parler face à face avec leurs amis.

Une chose est sûre: la vie de tous les jours est plus facile grâce à la technologie mais il faut que tout le monde reste conscient des dangers qui existent.

Section 2

Stéphanie: Salut, Germain. Comment ça va?

Germain: Très bien. Et toi, Stéphanie?

S: Super bien, merci. Je vais au cinéma ce soir car c'est mon anniversaire.

G: Qu'est-ce que vous allez voir?

S: Je crois que c'est une comédie.

G: Tu aimes bien les films marrants?

S: Oui, j'adore les films marrants. Mais je préfère les thrillers car j'aime le suspense et j'essaie de deviner qui est le tueur.

G: Alors, tu aimes aller au ciné?

S: Oui. C'est vraiment bien. J'aime l'ambiance du cinéma: il n'y a rien de mieux que de voir un film sur un grand écran et le son est toujours très clair.

G: Est-ce que tu regardes souvent la télé?

S: En ce moment, non. J'ai des examens cette année donc je passe beaucoup de temps à réviser ou à faire mes devoirs. Je dirais que je passe environ une heure par jour à regarder la télé.

G: Qu'est-ce que tu aimes regarder à la télé?

S: J'adore regarder les feuilletons. Ça m'aide à me détendre après une longue journée au lycée et je n'ai pas besoin de me concentrer. J'aime aussi les jeux télévisés car je trouve qu'on y apprend des choses et j'essaie de répondre aux questions.

G: Est-ce que tu aimes les émissions de télé-réalité?

S: Ça dépend lesquelles. J'aime bien « Masterchef ». C'est bien de voir les candidats progresser, ils font souvent de bonnes choses à manger et on peut essayer des recettes à la maison. C'est très intéressant.

G: Qu'est-ce que tu n'aimes pas regarder?

S: Je n'aime pas trop les émissions de sport. Je ne suis pas très sportive et je trouve ces émissions très ennuyeuses. Mais ce qui m'énerve le plus à la télé, c'est qu'il y a des publicités toutes les dix minutes et elles sont vraiment nulles.

G: Ah, c'est vrai. Tu as raison. Passe une bonne soirée au cinéma!

S: Merci. Tiens, est-ce que tu veux venir avec moi?

G: Je ne peux pas ce soir. Je dois aller au boulot. Merci quand même.

 **ACTIVITY:** 4. HOME AREA AND THE ENVIRONMENT – OÙ J'HABITE ET L'ENVIRONNEMENT (P100)

Section 1

Bonjour. Je m'appelle Michel et en ce moment je vis dans une grande ville dans le sud de la France. Ça fait huit ans que j'y habite et j'aime la vie en ville car on a tout à proximité et la vie nocturne est géniale. De plus, ma ville se trouve à dix minutes de la mer, ce qui est vraiment bien. J'y vais pratiquement chaque weekend pour promener mon chien et souvent à midi je mange dans un des nombreux restaurants sur la plage. Les seuls inconvénients de ma ville sont qu'il y a trop de touristes en été, beaucoup de déchets par terre et trop de pollution à cause des voitures.

Quand j'étais jeune, je vivais à la campagne mais à l'âge de dix-huit ans j'ai quitté mon village pour chercher du travail en ville. Je détestais la vie à la campagne car il n'y avait rien à faire pour les jeunes de mon âge. Par exemple, le cinéma le plus proche se trouvait à une heure de chez nous et il n'y avait pas de transport en commun non plus. Les seuls avantages à vivre à la campagne étaient qu'on pouvait jouer dehors en toute sécurité et que tout le monde se connaissait.

Ma femme vient de trouver du travail en Angleterre alors on va déménager à Manchester dans six semaines. Je suis assez content d'aller vivre en Angleterre car j'adore l'humour britannique et je pourrai améliorer mon anglais. Par contre je sais qu'il ne fera pas aussi beau qu'en France. Ha ha!

Section 2

Yannick:	Salut, Paula. Ça va?
Paula:	Oui, très bien. Je viens de passer le weekend chez mes grands-parents. Ils habitent un petit village à la montagne et c'était génial.
Y:	Sympa. Elle est comment, leur maison?
P:	Ils habitent une ferme. La maison de mes grands-parents est très grande donc j'ai ma propre chambre. En plus, ils ont une grande piscine ce qui est génial.
Y:	Et tu ne t'ennuies pas avec eux?
P:	Pas du tout. Mes grands-parents sont jeunes d'esprit donc je peux parler de tout avec eux. De plus, ma cousine, qui a le même âge que moi, habite la maison d'en face.
Y:	Mais qu'est-ce que tu as fait tout le weekend?
P:	Le samedi, on est allé faire quelques courses au marché et j'ai aidé mon grand-père à s'occuper des animaux. Et puis dimanche, comme il faisait super beau, on a fait un barbecue chez ma cousine.
Y:	Et elle a quel âge, ta cousine?
P:	Dix-sept ans.
Y:	Et elle aime y vivre toute l'année?
P:	Elle adore y vivre. Elle est très sportive, et donc en hiver elle peut skier et en été faire des randonnées. La seule chose qu'elle n'aime pas c'est qu'elle doit se lever très tôt le matin pour prendre le bus pour aller au lycée, qui se trouve à une heure de chez elle. Mais à part ça elle adore.
Y:	Et toi aussi apparemment?
P:	Oui, absolument. J'adore y aller car le paysage est vraiment beau. Quand je passe un weekend chez mes grands-parents, je me détends et je me sens beaucoup moins stressée. Tu devrais venir avec moi un de ces jours.
Y:	Peut-être - on verra!

 **ACTIVITY:** 5. EXPERIENCE AT SCHOOL AND FUTURE PLANS – LA VIE SCOLAIRE ET LES PROJETS POUR L'AVENIR (PP100–101)

Section 1

Moi, je fréquente un lycée qui se trouve assez près du centre-ville. C'est un assez grand lycée mais le bâtiment est très vieux. J'aime bien mon école car il y a une bonne ambiance et c'est animé. En plus il y a un bon rapport entre les profs et les élèves.

Malheureusement, je trouve que la journée à l'école est très fatigante. Les cours commencent à huit heures et ils finissent à seize heures, donc je passe huit heures au lycée. Et, en plus, quand je rentre à la maison, je passe au moins deux heures à faire mes devoirs. Ce que je trouve le plus difficile, c'est que je dois me réveiller à six heures trente parce que ma maison se trouve loin du lycée.

En ce qui concerne mes études, cette année je fais six matières et je vais passer mes examens au mois de juin. Ce que j'aime le plus, c'est le dessin. J'ai toujours de bonnes notes et je suis très créative. De plus mon prof de dessin nous inspire, il prépare bien ses cours et il explique tout clairement.

En général, les profs sont sympas, même si quelques-uns sont un peu sévères.

Section 2

```
Jérôme: Bonjour Sylvie. Ça va?
Sylvie: Oui. Ça va, merci.
J:      Est-ce que tu as des projets pour l'avenir?
S:      Oui, bien sûr. Après avoir passé mes examens, je voudrais me
        détendre et sortir avec mes amis pendant les grandes vacances.
        Puis, en septembre, j'ai l'intention de faire une formation
        pour devenir styliste pour créer des vêtements car je suis
        passionnée par la mode. D'ailleurs je dépense tout mon argent
        de poche en vêtements et en chaussures.
J:      Ah, oui. C'est intéressant. Est-ce que tu vas rester chez toi
        ou est-ce que tu vas chercher un appartement?
S:      Pendant la première année, je vais rester chez moi et habiter
        chez mes parents. Je n'ai pas assez d'argent pour me payer mon
        propre appartement et je n'ai pas de petit boulot. J'ai envie
        de trouver un boulot à mi-temps.
J:      Alors rester à la maison, ça ne te dérange pas?
S:      Mais non, pas du tout. J'ai de bonnes relations avec mes
        parents. Je dirais qu'on rigole et qu'on a plein de choses en
        commun. En plus, habiter avec ma mère a des avantages. C'est
        ma mère qui prépare les repas et qui fait la lessive, donc je
        ne peux pas me plaindre!
J:      Tu dois trouver un petit boulot, donc où est-ce que tu
        voudrais travailler?
S:      Si possible, j'aimerais travailler dans un magasin de
        vêtements. J'ai hâte de gagner un salaire. Je vais économiser
        mon argent pour pouvoir me trouver un appartement.
J:      Alors, en ce moment, tu n'as pas d'emploi. Pourquoi?
S:      Comme j'ai dit, j'ai beaucoup de travail cette année donc
        je me consacre à mes études. Ce n'est pas facile car je
        préférerais passer du temps avec mes amis. Nous adorons aller
        en ville pour faire les magasins ou bavarder dans les cafés.
        C'est amusant et nous pouvons oublier les soucis de l'école.
        D'ailleurs j'ai rendez-vous avec mes amis. Il faut que je m'en
        aille. À la prochaine!
J:      Très bien. À bientôt!
```

 **ACTIVITY** 6. JOB SEARCHES AND INTERVIEWS –
LA RECHERCHE D'EMPLOI ET LES
ENTRETIENS (P102)

Section 1

Alors, c'est le mois de juin et l'année scolaire est presque finie. Cet été, je ne pars pas en vacances et donc je vais rester chez moi. Mes parents disent que je devrais trouver un emploi à mi-temps. Comme ça je pourrai payer la facture de mon portable. Je pourrai aussi économiser pour mes études car je vais à l'université l'an prochain. Peut-être qu'ils ont raison mais on dit qu'il n'est pas facile de trouver un emploi pendant les vacances.

Depuis cinq semaines, je passe des heures à chercher un emploi à mi-temps. C'est affreux. Il n'y a que des annonces pour des secrétaires de bureau ou pour des serveurs dans les cafés ou les restaurants. Le problème, c'est que je n'ai pas l'expérience nécessaire et ces deux boulots ne m'intéressent pas du tout.

Mais le weekend dernier, j'ai trouvé une annonce pour un moniteur de tennis. C'est un boulot de rêve pour moi parce que je pourrai très souvent jouer au tennis. En plus je pourrais travailler avec des enfants et j'adore travailler en plein air. J'ai posé ma candidature pour ce poste et j'ai un entretien mardi prochain.

Section 2

Raphaël:	Bonjour, Christine. Ça va?
Christine:	Oui. Ça va, merci.
R:	Est-ce que tu es prête pour ton entretien?
C:	Pas encore mais j'ai l'intention de me préparer un peu. Pour commencer je vais faire des recherches en ligne pour me renseigner sur l'entreprise. Je vais aussi préparer des questions bien sûr.
R:	Ah, oui. Qu'est-ce que tu vas porter à l'entretien?
C:	Ma mère m'a conseillé de porter une jupe noire, un chemisier blanc et un pull noir.
R:	Bon, où est l'entretien exactement?
C:	Je crois que c'est dans un bureau au centre-ville, à environ quinze minutes en bus de ma maison. L'entretien commence à dix heures du matin donc je devrai quitter la maison vers neuf heures et demie. Je ne voudrais pas être en retard!
R:	Alors, tu vas gagner combien d'argent?
C:	Je pense que je serai payée neuf euros de l'heure. C'est très bien payé, non?
R:	Oui, c'est vrai. Tu devras travailler combien d'heures par semaine?
C:	L'annonce dit que l'employé doit travailler quatre jours par semaine, huit heures par jour. La pause déjeuner dure quarante-cinq minutes. J'aurai assez de temps libre et plus d'argent pour sortir avec mes copains.
R:	Est-ce que l'annonce décrit la personne idéale pour ce boulot?
C:	Oui. Évidemment, ils cherchent une personne qui sait travailler en équipe, qui est ponctuelle et à qui on peut faire confiance.
R:	À ton avis, quels sont les avantages de trouver un boulot pendant les vacances?
C:	Pour moi, il y a plusieurs avantages à travailler pendant les vacances. À mon avis, les plus importants sont de gagner mon propre argent, de devenir plus indépendante et de me faire de nouveaux amis. J'aimerais vraiment obtenir ce boulot et j'espère réussir à l'entretien.
R:	Je te souhaite bonne chance! À bientôt.

⚙ ACTIVITY: 7. HOLIDAYS – LES VACANCES (P101)

Section 1

Chaque année, je passe les grandes vacances chez ma tante. J'y vais avec mes parents et ma sœur cadette et on y passe un mois. Ma tante habite un petit village à quinze km de Toulouse dans le sud-ouest de la France. Elle a une maison à trois étages avec quatre chambres et deux salles de bains. J'adore y aller car c'est tranquille et c'est l'occasion de me détendre après une année chargée au lycée.

Mais ce que j'aime le plus c'est de pouvoir passer du temps avec Anne, ma cousine. On s'entend super bien, on a le même âge, elle est vraiment marrante et on peut discuter de tout ensemble.

Je passe presque tout mon temps avec Anne. Normalement, on passe les journées à se baigner dans la piscine ou on fait des randonnées à vélo dans la campagne. S'il fait vraiment trop chaud on reste à la maison et on joue aux cartes.

Le seul inconvénient de partir en vacances, c'est que je dois laisser mon chien avec ma grand-mère à Paris et qui il me manque beaucoup. Mais il est toujours très content quand je rentre.

Section 2

Laure:	Bonjour, Cédric. Comment ça va?
Cédric:	Je suis un peu triste car je viens de rentrer de vacances. J'ai passé quinze jours en Espagne.
L:	Avec qui y es-tu allé?
C:	J'y suis allé avec quatre copains du lycée. C'est la première fois que je partais en vacances sans mes parents et c'était génial. On pouvait se lever tard le matin, manger ce qu'on voulait et aller en boîte sans demander la permission.
L:	Super. Alors tout s'est bien passé?
C:	En fait, ça a mal commencé. D'abord, l'avion avait deux heures de retard et ensuite la compagnie aérienne a perdu nos bagages. Heureusement, on les a retrouvés le lendemain de notre arrivée. Mais ensuite tout s'est bien passé.
L:	Où avez-vous logé?
C:	On a logé dans un hôtel trois étoiles qui se trouvait juste en face de la mer. J'ai partagé une chambre avec mon meilleur ami alors on a bien rigolé. La chambre était très propre et bien équipée.
L:	Qu'avez-vous fait?
C:	Ben... la première semaine, on n'a pas fait grand-chose à part se baigner dans la mer et jouer au volley sur la plage. Mais la deuxième semaine, on a fait quelques excursions. Comme on s'intéresse tous à l'histoire, on a visité de vieilles églises et des villages typiques. C'était vraiment très intéressant.
L:	Avez-vous bien mangé?
C:	Ah, oui. On a très bien mangé. Tous les repas étaient délicieux et vraiment pas chers. On a surtout adoré les tapas.
L:	Recommanderais-tu l'Espagne alors?
C:	Absolument. D'abord, il y fait un temps splendide, les gens sont très accueillants et en plus ça donne l'occasion d'améliorer son espagnol et de rencontrer de nouvelles personnes.

APPENDICES

ANSWERS
SOCIETY

Family and friends – La famille et les amis 2 (pp8–9)

 **ACTIVITY:** Negatives – Les négatifs

My older brother is not patient.

My mum is never lively.

My dad is no longer annoying, he listens to me.

My younger sister is only fun with her friends.

No one is understanding at home.

My older sister is not generous, she doesn't give me anything.

Relationships – Les relations (pp10–11)

 **ACTIVITY:** Positive relationships – Les rapports positifs

on s'intéresse aux mêmes choses –we are interested in the same things

on partage les mêmes intérêts – we share the same interests

on a beaucoup de choses en commun – we have a lot of things in common

il/elle a un bon sens de l'humour – he/she has a good sense of humour

on passe beaucoup de temps ensemble – we spend a lot of time together

on fait tout ensemble – we do everything together

on sort souvent ensemble – we often go out together

on partage de bons moments – we share good times together

il/elle est toujours de bonne humeur – he/she is always in a good mood

on rigole – we have a laugh

on peut discuter de tout – we can discuss everything

il/elle me respecte – he/she respects me

on est très proche – we are very close

il/elle est très respectueux (-euse) de ma vie privée – he/she is very respectful of my private life

il/elle m'aide quand j'en ai besoin – he/she helps me when I need it

il/elle me soutient quand j'ai un problème – he/she supports me when I have a problem

 **ACTIVITY:** Parental relationships – Les relations avec ses parents

1. sorth, amis = My parents let me go out with my friends every weekend.

2. liberté – My parents give me enough freedom

3. donnent, poche – My parents give me a lot of pocket money.

4. respectueux; privée – My parents are very respectful of my private life.

5. m'entends; confiance – I get on well with my parents because they trust me.

6. compréhensifs; conseils – My parents are very understanding and they give me good advice.

7. proche; discuter – I am very close to my parents because we can discuss everything.

8. discute; s'intéresse – I am lucky because I discuss everything with my parents and we are interested in the same things.

9. humeur; rigole – My mum is always in a good mood and we have a laugh together.

Family conflicts – Les conflits familiaux 1 (pp12–13)

 **ACTIVITY:** Negative relationships 1 – Les rapports négatifs 1

1. I have a bad relationship with my sister.

2. I have a bad relationship with my grandmother.

3. I get on badly with my uncle.

4. I don't get on well with my brother.

5. I often argue with my parents.

6. From time to time there are tensions with my parents.

 **ACTIVITY:** Adverbs – Les adverbes

1. Always		4.	From time to time
2. Often		5.	Rarely
3. Sometimes			

Rule for adverbs of frequency: Adverbs of frequency are usually placed after the verb. Parfois is placed at the start of the sentence.

 **ACTIVITY:** Negative relationships 2 – Les rapports négatifs 2

1. my dad/my mum/my brother/my sister is

2. my parents are

3. he/ she is

4. they are

5. he/she takes my clothes without asking permission

6. he/she lies all the time

7. my parents want to watch different programmes on TV

8. he/she listens to music too loudly when I am doing my homework

9. they change their behaviour in front of my parents

10. my dad makes fun of me in front of my friends

11. my brother teases me all the time

12. my sister uses my make-up/my computer without asking me for permission

THINGS TO DO AND THINK ABOUT

I argue with my parents because of

... studies

- They think I don't study enough.
- They are not happy with my marks at school.

...going out

- They don't let me go out with my friends during the week.
- They don't give me enough freedom.

... my friends

... my boyfriend/girlfriend

- They don't like my friends/ boyfriend/girlfriend.
- They think I spend too much time with my friends.
- They believe I am too young to have a boyfriend/girlfriend.

... money

- They don't give me enough money.
- They think I waste my money.

- They won't let me find a part time job to earn some money.

... housework

- They think that I don't do anything at home and that I am too lazy.
- I believe that I help a lot at home but they don't agree.
- I have to do a lot of housework but my brother doesn't do anything.

... my private life

- They interfere with my things.
- They don't respect my private life.

- They always want to know what is happening in my life which annoys me.
- They ask too many questions about my friends/boyfriend/girlfriend/studies.

... my behaviour

- They think that I am disobedient.
- They are not happy about my behaviour at home/school.

... my hobbies

- They think I spend too much time watching TV/listening to music/playing on the computer.
- They say that I spend too much time on the internet/on my mobile phone/on Facebook.

Family conflicts - Les conflits familiaux 2 (pp14–15)

 **ACTIVITY:** Arguments with parents 1 – Les disputes avec ses parents 1

	Jérôme	Marianne
Who does he/ she argue with ?	His dad	Her mum
Why?	• His dad is always nagging him. • His dad thinks he is always on his mobile phone. • His dad doesn't like his girlfriend. • His dad thinks he is too young to have a girlfriend. • His dad thinks he should spend more time studying. • His dad interferes with his things. • His dad doesn't respect his private life.	• Her mum criticises her all the time. • Her mum tells her off for not doing the dishes or the vacuuming. • Her brother doesn't do anything. • Her friends get £20 each week without helping at home. • She wouldn't get any pocket money if she didn't do the housework. • She only gets £10 per week which is not enough for her.

Ideal parents - Les parents idéaux (pp16–17)

 **ACTIVITY:** Conditional tense – Le conditionnel

1. Je regarderais la télé avec mon père.
2. Je finirais mes devoirs.
3. Je lirais un livre.
4. Nous passerions/on passerait plus de temps ensemble.
5. Nous parlerions/on parlerait plus souvent.

 **ACTIVITY:** Irregular conditional stems – Les verbes irréguliers au conditionnel

1. J'irais au cinéma avec ma mère le weekend.
2. Mon père serait plus patient.
3. Mes parents auraient plus de temps libre.
4. Je ferais du sport avec mon père.
5. Je pourrais sortir avec mes amis en semaine.

 **ACTIVITY:** An ideal parent – Un parent idéal 1

5. An ideal parent would be patient and tolerant.
7. An ideal parent would always be available to help their children.
11. An ideal parent would trust their children.
1. An ideal parent would allow their children to have enough freedom.
8. An ideal parent would spend a lot of time with their children.
3. An ideal parent would protect their children.
9. An ideal parent would give good advice to their children.
6. An ideal parent would not be old fashioned.
4. An ideal parent would not be too protective.
10. An ideal parent would never spoil their children.
2. An ideal parent would not get easily annoyed.

Friendship - L'amitié (pp18–19)

 **ACTIVITY:** Spending time with your family/friends – Passer du temps avec sa famille/ses amis

meilleure; intérêts; magasins; rigole; comiques; partie; j'aime; samedi; drôle; s'intéresse; télé; m'aide; conseils; longueur d'onde; confiance

 **ACTIVITY:** Relationships with friends – Les rapports avec les amis

A good friend:

1. He/she understands me.
2. He/she doesn't criticise me.
6. He/she is not annoying.
7. He/she is never jealous.
9. He/she has a sense of humour.
11. He/she is not selfish.
12. He/she respects me.
14. I can confide in him/her.
16. He/she is always there when I need someone.

A bad friend:

3. He/she rarely encourages me.
4. He/she never supports me.
5. He/she annoys me/gets on my nerves.
8. He/she bores me.
10. He/she complains all the times.
13. He/she never listens to me.
15. He/she ignores me at school.
17. He/she argues about anything.

 **ACTIVITY:** Translating the conditional tense

1. Il/elle me comprendrait.
2. Il/elle ne me critiquerait pas.
3. Il/elle m'encouragerait rarement.
4. Il/elle ne me soutiendrait jamais.
5. Il/elle m'énerverait.
6. Il/elle ne serait pas embêtant(e).
7. Il/elle ne serait jamais jaloux(-se).
8. Il/elle m' ennuierait.
9. Il/elle aurait le sens de l'humour.
10. Il/elle se plaindrait tout le temps.
11. Il/elle ne serait pas égoïste.
12. Il/elle me respecterait.
13. Il/elle ne m'écouterait jamais.
14. Je pourrais me confier à lui/elle.
15. Il/elle m'ignorerait à l'école.
16. Il/elle serait toujours là quand j'ai besoin de quelqu'un.
17. Il/elle se disputerait pour n'importe quoi.

 **ACTIVITY:** Peer pressure – L'influence des pairs

1. YES	6. YES	11. YES	16. YES
2. NO	7. YES	12. YES	17. NO
3. YES	8. NO	13. YES	18. YES
4. YES	9. NO	14. NO	
5. NO	10. YES	15. YES	

THINGS TO DO AND THINK ABOUT

- to need
- to want
- to be scared
- to have the opportunity
- to be lucky
- to have trouble/difficulty
- to seem
- to be thirsty
- to be hungry
- to be hot
- to be cold

Leisure – Les loisirs 1 (pp22–23)

 **ACTIVITY:** Revision – La révision

My favourite hobby is...
- to play tennis
- to go swimming
- reading
- to go to the cinema
- to go shopping
- to watch TV
- to do horse riding
- to go shopping.

Who with?
- With my friends
- With my dad/my mum
- I am a member of a club
- I am part of a team
- Alone

When?
- On Saturday morning
- On Tuesday after lessons
- On Wednesday evening
- On Sunday afternoon
- Once a week
- Three times a month
- Often
- Sometimes

- From time to time
- Rarely

Where?
- At the park
- At the football pitch/golf course
- In the town centre
- At home
- At the sports centre
- In the garden

Opinions?
- I love
- I like
- ... excites me
- ... interests me

Why?
- It is fun
- It is exciting
- It is entertaining
- It is relaxing
- I can meet new people
- It helps me to relax
- It's a way of escaping the stress of school life
- It's good for your health
- It keeps me fit

 **ACTIVITY:** Hobbies – Les passe-temps

- To do horse riding
- To go shopping
- To do cycling
- To do mountain biking
- To go swimming
- To go hiking
- To do sailing
- To do wind-surfing
- To do diving
- To go horse riding
- To do water sports
- To go shopping

- To go for a walk
- To go for a bike ride/a boat trip
- To swim
- To read novels
- To go out with my friends
- To spend time with my friends
- To go to a party/a night club
- To go the cinema/theatre
- To go to the swimming pool
- To watch TV/films
- To listen to music on my iPod
- To spend hours on the internet/on Facebook
- To chat to my friends on my mobile phone
- To visit someone

Leisure – Les loisirs 2 (pp24–25)

ACTIVITY: To do sport – Faire du sport

1. Je fais du vélo.
2. Il fait du VTT.
3. Elle fait de la natation.
4. Nous faisons/On fait de la randonnée.
5. Ils font de l'équitation/du cheval.
6. Je fais de la planche à voile.
7. Vous faites de la voile.
8. Elles font des sports aquatiques.

ACTIVITY: To go to the ... – Aller au/à la/à l'/aux...

1. Je vais au cinéma.
2. Il va au centre sportif.
3. Elle va à la plage.
4. Nous allons/On va aux magasins.
5. Ils vont au théâtre.
6. Je vais au centre commercial.
7. Vous allez au restaurant.
8. Elles vont à l'hôtel.

ACTIVITY: Opinions – Les opinions

Opinion phrases:
- Je crois que
- J'adore
- Mon sport préféré, c'est
- Ce que j'aime le plus, c'est
- Je pense que
- Elle préfère
- Elle dit que
- Elle adore ça
- Selon moi
- J'ai horreur de
- Je trouve ça ennuyeux
- Mon père s'intéresse au
- Il croit que
- Ma mère déteste
- Elle préfère
- Ce que je trouve.
- Elle préférerait
- Elle pense que

Hobbies:

Jacques – playing basketball with his friends because they have fun and he enjoys playing in a team

Sister – swimming because it keeps her fit

Dad – watching sport on TV because it helps him to relax after spending the day at work

Mum – watching romantic films on TV/ prefers reading a good novel as it is an escape from everyday life

Healthy Lifestyles – La vie saine 1 (pp26–27)

ACTIVITY: Healthy living

Pierre:

1. Pierre thinks we must have a balanced diet to satisfy our nutritional needs.
2. We should avoid fatty food like pizza, chips and crisps, and sugary foods like chocolate as you can become obese.
3. Obesity can lead to illnesses like diabetes and heart disease.
4. Meat and fish provide us with iron and protein,
5. Fruit and vegetables provide us with fibre, vitamins and minerals.
6. Pierre mentions milk and cheese.

7. Water is essential for hydration and you should drink at least 2 litres of water per day.

8. You should avoid drinking too much caffeine and alcohol.

Thérèse:

1. Thérèse likes fatty foods and sugary foods (like chocolate and sweets).

2. She likes to drink fizzy drinks.

3. She eats a lot of snacks to console herself as she is under a lot of pressure at school this year.

4. She feels depressed because she is putting on weight.

5. She has started skipping meals in order to lose weight.

6. She can't concentrate at school due to tiredness and lack of sleep.

7. She likes McDonalds because the service is quick and it isn't expensive.

8. Her mum thinks fast food is not good for your health and fatty products, like hamburgers and chips, have too many calories.

Healthy lifestyle – La vie saine 2 (pp28–29)

 **ACTIVITY:** Keeping fit

Alain: l'exercice physique; alimentaire; depuis; compétitif; terrain de golf; jouer; continuer; les écrans; garder.

Brigitte: active; me détend; gymnase; basket; à pied; l'escalier; ascenseur; maladies; obèse; l'intention.

Antoine: natation; l'entraînement; concours; c'était; me lever; piscine; me coucher; l'équilibre; malade.

 **ACTIVITY:** The simple future tense – Le futur simple

1. Je passerai moins de temps à regarder la télé.

2. Je mangerai sainement.

3. Je jouerai au foot avec mes amis.

4. Nous boirons/on boira deux litres d'eau par jour.

5. Nous éviterons/on évitera les matières grasses.

 **ACTIVITY:** Irregular verbs in the simple future tense – Les irréguliers au futur simple

1. J'irai au gymnase.

2. Je ferai plus de sport.

3. Je devrai faire plus d'exercice physique.

4. Nous pourrons/on pourra rester en bonne forme.

5. Nous serons/on sera plus actif(s).

Lifestyle related illnesses – Les maladies (pp30–31)

 **ACTIVITY:** Smoking and alcohol – Le tabac et l'alcool

People who smoke or drink alcohol:

2. I drink alcohol because it gives me self-confidence.

4. I drink alcohol because it helps me to escape from worries about everyday life.

7. I drink alcohol because I don't want to be different from my friends.

9. I smoke because it helps me to relax.

10. I drink alcohol because all my friends drink alcohol.

11. I smoke because it is a habit and it is my choice.

12. I drink alcohol because it helps me to feel at ease.

15. I smoke because I think it looks cool.

17. All my problems disappear when I drink alcohol.

19. I smoke because it helps me to relax when I am stressed.

People who don't smoke or don't drink alcohol:

1. I don't drink alcohol because it is not good for your health.

3. I no longer smoke because it is too expensive.

5. I don't smoke because it is harmful for your health.

6. I never drink alcohol because it has a negative effect on your behaviour.

8. I don't drink alcohol because my parents would no longer trust me.

13. I don't smoke because there is the risk of addiction.

14. I don't drink alcohol because my parents would be angry.

16. Even though I am surrounded by people who smoke, I don't want to smoke because it is dangerous for your health.

18. I never smoke because I am scared that I would not be able to stop.

20. I don't drink alcohol because I don't like the taste and I don't smoke because it smells bad.

 **ACTIVITY:** Why do people smoke or drink alcohol? – Pourquoi est-ce qu'on fume ou boit de l'alcool?

Frédéric: amis; fument; l'air; heureux; aide; risques.

Sandrine: l'alcool; un verre; confiance; régulièrement; ivres; comportement.

Jean-Luc: offert; drogue; essayant; dépendant; surdose; colère.

Television – La télé (pp32–33)

1. (m) News

2. (b) Documentaries (about nature/history)

3. (j) Sports/ music programmes

4. (o) Cartoons

5. (a) Soaps

6. (h) A game show

7. (c) Adverts

8. (p) The weather

9. (l) A western

10. (q) A comedy

11. (e) An adventure film

12. (i) A war film

13. (f) A science-fiction film

14. (n) A crime film

15. (r) A spy film

16. (g) A thriller

17. (k) A horror film

18. (d) A romantic film

Watching TV – Regarder la télé (pp34–35)

 **ACTIVITY:** Opinions of different programmes – Les opinions des émissions différentes

Sandra: écran; feuilletons; divertissants; me détendre.

Anna: perte; sans arrêt; documentaires; m'informent.

Christophe: en semaine; policiers; passionnants; jeux télévisés.

Simon: la météo; communiquer; monde; frappant.

Céline: accro; rate; bête ; paresseuse.

APPENDICES

 **ACTIVITY**: Preceding Direct Objects

1. J'aime les westerns. Je les regarde souvent.

2. J'adore les comédies. Je les regarde le weekend.

3. Je n'aime pas les documentaires. Je les regarde rarement.

4. Je n'aime pas le foot. Je le regarde de temps en temps.

5. J'aime la météo. Je la regarde tous les jours.

6. Je déteste les films policiers. Je ne les regarde jamais.

Reality TV - La télé-réalité (pp36-37)

 **ACTIVITY**: For or against reality TV - Pour ou contre la télé réalité

1. It made him laugh/he found it entertaining.

2. It is a recent phenomenon/it has become more popular over the last few years/it doesn't do anything useful for society.

3. It is difficult to escape them/there are too many on TV.

4. It is a competition where people want to seize the opportunity to win a big prize or be famous/your dreams can come true like become a famous singer.

5. He votes for his favourite (he wants them to win).

6. The candidates doing silly things/it is shocking/embarrassing.

7. Reality TV is a bad influence on children and young people.

8. Life is easy/all you need to do to be rich and famous is to participate in a reality TV programme/they don't have to work hard to succeed.

9. People who do a lot of things to help others in society/people who have a positive influence on society.

10. Observing the relationships between people/observing people's reactions.

Technology - La technologie (pp38-39)

 **ACTIVITY**: Use of technology - L'usage de la technologie

- J'envoie des SMS/des textos à mes amis avec mon portable – I send text messages to my friends

- Je réserve des places de concerts en ligne – I reserve seats for concerts on line

- Je peux télécharger des films et de la musique – I can download films and music

- Je fais des recherches pour mes devoirs – I do research for my homework

- Je prends des photos car mon portable a un appareil photo intégré – I take photos because my mobile phone has an integrated camera

- Je commande des livres en ligne – I order books online

- Je surfe sur le net pour m'informer – I surf on the internet

- J'envoie des emails – I send emails

- J'utilise l'Internet pour écouter de la musique ou regarder les films – I use the internet to listen to music or watch films

- Je tchate dans les forums pour rencontrer des amis – I chat on forums to meet friends

- Je fais du shopping en ligne – I do shopping online

- Je reste en contact avec mes cousins à l'étranger grâce au net – I stay in contact with my cousins abroad through the net

- Je retire de l'argent au distributeur automatique – I take money out of the cash machine

- Mes parents achètent les billets d'avion et réservent un hôtel pour les vacances sur le net – my parents buy the plane tickets and reserve a hotel for the holidays on the net

- Je joue à des jeux en ligne – I play games on line

 **ACTIVITY**: Advantages and disadvantages of technology – Les avantages et les inconvénients de la technologie

Advantages:

1. It simplifies life. You can stay in contact with your friends and parents from anywhere.

3. I do everything on the internet. I buy clothes, I download music and films online which is cheaper than CDs & DVDs.

4. Technology is a good thing. My favourite site is Facebook as I can communicate with friends. It is quick and you can see friends' photos immediately. You can express your ideas and opinions.

6. You can compare prices online. There is more choice online than in the shops. At Christmas, I look for presents which are bargains/ a good price/ inexpensive.

10. Technology is a good thing. I can escape and lose myself by listening to music on my iPod without disturbing anyone. I can also read all sorts of books on the same screen.

Disadvantages:

2. Technology is not a good thing. It is expensive. It is a waste of money. Using a mobile can be dangerous for your health.

5. Social networking sites can be dangerous. You can meet strange people when you chat online. There are people who manipulate young people and who hide behind their computer screens.

7. Technology is a bad thing. I don't like reading books or listening to music on the internet. I prefer to buy real books and CDs in a shop. I don't understand the language of technology.

8. Technology is a bad thing. There are dangers on the net. Young people can be victims to intimidation by receiving threatening and insulting messages from other people. Parents worry about the safety of their children.

9. Technology is a bad thing. We are too dependent on our mobile phone. We send text messages, we speak to friends, we read books, we surf the net, we play games and we listen to music. We spend too much time on our mobile phones. Communication breaks down between people. It has a negative effect on relationships. Some people cannot live without their mobiles.

Your home area as a tourist area - Ta region comme lieu touristique (pp40-41)

 **ACTIVITY**: Where you live – Là où tu habites

(a) 1. à   3. en   5. au

    2. aux   4. à   6. en

(b)

Le nord

Le nord-ouest   Le nord-est

L'ouest   Le Centre   L'est

Le sud-ouest   Le sud-est

Le sud

(c) 1. A.   3. F.   5. H.   7. E.

    2. D.   4. G.   6. B.   8. C.

 **ACTIVITY:** Describing your area – Décrire ton quartier

Positif

- agréable
- amusant(e)
- animé(e)
- beau/belle
- ancien(ne)
- historique
- industriel(le)
- joli(e)
- magnifique
- moderne
- pittoresque
- propre
- touristique
- tranquille

Négatif

- pollué(e)

 **ACTIVITY:** My home town – Ma ville

A. grande ville; nord-est; industrielle; animée.

B. petit village; centre; tranquille.

C. au bord de la mer; sud-ouest; propre; touristique.

A tourist town - Une ville touristique (pp42–43)

 **ACTIVITY:** My town – Ma ville

Philippe:

1. A small, picturesque village at the seaside.
2. *Any three from:* Go for a walk on the beach/stroll in the town to see the beautiful buildings/do water sports/do wind-surfing/do diving/hire boats.
3. In a youth hostel.
4. The small, typical restaurants because the food is delicious.

Sandrine:

1. A fun city.
2. There are lots of things to do and to see.
3. *Any three from: A*n old castle/lots of historic monuments/museums/galleries.
4. See a show at the theatre/go to concerts.
5. Discover tourist sites on a tourist bus which tours the city.
6. A bowling alley/an ice rink/a large public park.
7. 4 & 5 star hotels/hire luxury apartments.

Jean-Luc:

8. In a village in the mountains.
9. Hike/ski.
10. In a 3 star hotel (on the main street).
11. In pubs/a traditional restaurant.
12. *Any one from:* There is not a lot to do in the evening/there is no cinema or theatre.
13. People come from other countries to his village/there are traditional music festivals.

Marie-Claire:

14. In the suburbs (outskirts)/a dynamic city/a multicultural city.
15. It is full of tourists throughout the year/there is a lively atmosphere.
16. Shop for (buy) souvenirs/eat in good traditional restaurants/go sight-seeing.
17. Lakes/mountains/(Scottish) distilleries.
18. It is easy to get around/there is a good public transport system.
19. Hotels/youth hostels/guest houses.

Town and country - La ville et la campagne 1 (pp44–45)

 **ACTIVITY:** Description of the town and the countryside - La description de la ville et de la campagne

- Tranquille – quiet (countryside)
- Cosmopolite – cosmopolitan (town)
- Calme – calm/quiet (countryside)
- Beau/belle – beautiful (town/countryside)
- Pollué(e) – polluted (town)
- Reposant(e) – relaxing (countryside)
- Stressant(e) – stressful (town)
- Animé(e) – lively (town)
- Ennuyeux/ ennuyeuse – boring (countryside)
- Divertissant(e) – entertaining (town)
- Vert(e) – green (countryside)
- Bruyant(e) – noisy (town)
- Isolé(e) – isolated (countryside)
- Cher/chère – expensive (town/countryside)
- Sale – dirty (town)

 **ACTIVITY:** The town - La ville

Les avantages:

3. There are a lot of things to do and see.
4. You can go sightseeing by visiting historic monuments and tourist sites.
6. There is a good choice of restaurants.
8. We can go shopping in the town centre.
9. The night life is great.
10. You can go out to a night-club.
11. There are a lot of opportunities to do sport.
14. You can get around easily because of the public transport system.
16. There is plenty of entertainment for young people.
18. You can make the most of the cultural life like the theatre and museums.

Les inconvénients:

1. It's noisy.
2. There is a lot of pollution.
5. There is a lot of litter on the ground.
7. There is too much traffic.
12. There are too many people.
13. The rents are high.
15. There are not enough green spaces.
17. Life can be stressful.
19. You don't know your neighbours.
20. You don't always feel safe.

ACTIVITY: The countryside – La campagne

Les avantages:

3. The landscape is beautiful.
5. The lifestyle is relaxing.
6. Everyone knows each other.
9. You are not stressed/rushed.
11. There are plenty of green spaces.

12. It is quite clean.

13. It is quiet and peaceful.

15. The air is pure because there is less pollution.

16. You can go for long walks.

17. You can relax.

18. You live close to nature.

20. There is less violence.

Les inconvénients:

1. You are isolated.

2. There is nothing for young people to do.

4. It is necessary to have a car to get around.

7. Life can be boring and monotonous.

8. You must go to town to study because there are no schools or universities.

10. There are no distractions.

14. There are no amenities nearby.

19. There are few possibilities to find a good job.

21. You live far from your friends.

22. Everyone is too interested in other people's lives.

23. There is less noise.

24. Public transport is not efficient.

Town and Country – La ville et la campagne 2 (pp46–47)

 **ACTIVITY** Comparative and superlative

1. La ville est plus amusante que la campagne.

2. La ville est moins ennuyeuse que la campagne.

3. La ville est la plus amusante.

4. La ville est la plus ennuyeuse.

5. La ville est la moins ennuyeuse.

6. La campagne est la moins amusante.

7. La ville est la meilleure.

8. La campagne est la pire.

 **ACTIVITY** Town or countryside – La ville ou la campagne

Corine:

1. She used to live in the countryside.

2. Everyone knew each other/they had a lot of freedom/you could play outside when the weather was nice/there were a lot of green spaces.

3. She now lives in a city/big town.

4. All her friends live near her/it is easy to get around/there is always something to do like go to the shopping centre or the cinema.

5. She would live in town because it is more lively than the countryside/there is a huge amount of distractions for young people.

Bernard:

1. He used to live in a town.

2. You could get around easily/there were a lot of distractions.

3. In the countryside.

4. There is less violence/you feel safer/he likes living close to nature/he likes spending his free time hiking.

5. The countryside/he loves the tranquillity and the peaceful way of life/he didn't like life in town because there were too many people, too much pollution and too much noise.

Delphine:

1. She used to live at the seaside.

2. Life was really exciting/there were always a lot of things to do/they spent weekends at the beach, going for long walks, doing water sports like wind surfing or playing volleyball.

3. The countryside.

4. There are no tourists in summer/there is less traffic.

5. In a town/she wants to go to university (to study foreign languages).

Environment – L'environnement (pp48–49)

 **ACTIVITY** Problems with the environment – Les problèmes de l'environnement

Problem 1. Deforestation

Solution 4. We must plant trees

Problem 2. Global warming and climatic change

Solution 8. We must use renewable energy and reduce the production of carbon dioxide

Problem 3. Air pollution because of vehicles

Solution 1. We must use unleaded petrol

Problem 4. Traffic and traffic jams

Solution 3. We must walk or use public transport

Problem 5. Drought

Solution 6. We must reduce the consumption of water by turning off the tap and by taking a shower instead of a bath

Problem 6. The extinction of endangered species

Solution 2. We must protect endangered species, for example the animals who live in the rainforest

Problem 7. The greenhouse effect and the hole in the ozone layer

Solution 5. We must limit the use of CFCs

Problem 8. Acid rain because of industrial activity

Solution 11. We must reduce factory emissions and the consumption of fossil fuels

Problem 9. Rubbish/waste

Solution 9. We must reduce rubbish and avoid wastage

Problem 10. Packaging

Solution 6. We must separate rubbish and recycle paper, plastic and glass

Problem 11. Waste of energy

Solution 12. We must conserve energy and use clean, renewable energy, like solar energy, or energy produced by wind or water

Problem 12. Water pollution

Solution 10. We must avoid throwing rubbish into the sea

 **ACTIVITY** Modal verbs – Les verbes modaux

1. Recycler
2. Acheter
3. Réutiliser
4. Réduire
5. Utiliser
6. Aller
7. Éteindre
8. Gaspiller
9. Protéger
10. Prendre

LEARNING

School Subjects – Les Matières (pp50–51)

 **ACTIVITY:** Learning activities – Les activités d'apprentissage

1. To learn vocabulary
2. To solve problems
3. To work alone
4. To work in a group/in a team
5. To work in pairs
6. To work on the computer
7. To copy notes from the board
8. To watch documentaries
9. To read
10. To look up words in the dictionary
11. To do research
12. To write essays
13. To create
14. To draw
15. To do homework
16. To do presentations
17. To play instruments
18. To do sorts activities
19. To participate in games
20. To listen to the teacher
21. To communicate with classmates
22. To do arithmetic and algebra
23. To do manuel work and DIY
24. To cook
25. To learn grammar
26. To learn to spell
27. To sit exams (oral/written)
28. To do scientific experiments

 **ACTIVITY:** What do you like doing at school/college or university? Qu'est-ce que tu aimes faire au lycée/ à la fac?

Name	Subject	Activities they enjoy	Reason	Activities they dislike	Reason
Frédéric	Spanish	Working in pairs Working in groups Speaking Spanish	Communicating (in Spanish)	Writing essays Learning grammar	Boring Difficult
Corinne	Science/ Biology	Working in pairs Doing experiments	Interesting	Doing research on the internet	Not easy to read and understand a lot of scientific articles
Thierry	Maths	Working alone Solving problems (in arithmetic & algebra)	Good at it Quite easy	Sitting exams	Doesn't like the pressure Gets nervous
Anna	PE	Being part of a team Participating in sports games	Fun Good to keep fit	Doing homework Writing essays	Boring Would prefer to spend time doing sporty and physical activities

Preparing for exams 1 – Se préparer aux examens (pp52–53)

 **ACTIVITY:** Passer les examens – To sit exams

1. This year I am sitting my National 5 exams.
2. I study six subjects, including maths, English, French, history, music and biology.
3. I am in the middle of preparing for my National 5 exams.
4. I am going to sit my National 5 exams at the end of the school year.
5. I would like to pass my exams this year as I intend to continue my studies next year.
6. If I get good grades, I will be able to find a good job in the future.
7. I have to do a lot of work to pass my exams.
8. I have to work hard to pass my exams because I want to leave school and find a good job.

 **ACTIVITY:** The exams – Les examens

1. I have written and oral exams.
2. I have to sit listening exams.
3. I have to read texts.
4. I have to do presentations.
5. I have to answer questions.
6. We must write essays.
7. We must do experiments.
8. We must do arithmatic.
9. We must cook a meal.
10. I have to play the guitar/I have to sing.
11. I have to draw pictures.
12. I have to make something/do DIY.
13. We need to solve problems.
14. We must do sport.
15. We must work on the computer.

 **ACTIVITY:** Preparations – Les préparations

1. E
2. F
3. G
4. K
5. B
6. H
7. A
8. C
9. D
10. J
11. I

Preparing for exams 2 – Se preparer aux examens (pp54–55)

 **ACTIVITY:** The pressure of exams – La pression des examens

1. Benjamin
2. Laure
3. Laure
4. Benjamin
5. Laure's
6. Benjamin's
7. Benjamin
8. Laure
9. Laure
10. Benjamin
11. Laure

1. Il y a beaucoup de pression.
2. C'est ma responsabilité.
3. Mes parents sont toujours sur mon dos.
4. Je dois réussir à mes examens.
5. Je préférerais passer mon temps...
6. Trouver l'équilibre entre les études et les loisirs...
7. Je trouve les révisions insupportables et vraiment ennuyeuses.
8. Ça peut être stressant.
9. Je me consacre à mes études.
10. Je n'ai pas l'intention de continuer.
11. On peut mieux se concentrer si on se sent bien.
12. Je fais de mon mieux.

Different education systems – Les systèmes scolaires différents (pp56–57)

APPENDICES

 **ACTIVITY:** The school system – Le système scolaire

Questions	Isabelle	Pierre	Mélanie
Where is the school?	Québec	Dakar/Senegal	Charleroi/Belgium
What size is it?	Average/ medium size	Big	Small
How many pupils are there?	955 pupils	1800 pupils	550 pupils
What is the building like?	Modern/ well equipped	Old building/old fashioned	Small/modern
How do they get to school?	By bike	Walk/on foot	School bus (free)
What time do lessons start and finish?	8.15am/2.40pm (08:00/14:40)	8am/5pm (08:00/17:00)	8.20am/ 4.15pm (08:00/16:15)
How many classes do they have per day and how long does each class last?	Four lessons per day. Each lesson lasts one and a quarter hours.	Four lessons per day. Each lesson lasts two hours.	Six lessons per day. Each lessons lasts 55 minutes. No lessons on Wednesday afternoon.
What time is lunch?	12.30pm	Midday	12.45pm
How long is the lunch break?	50 minutes	One hour	One hour and ten minutes
Where do they eat lunch?	Canteen	Home	Canteen
What is their opinion of the canteen?	The food is healthy/ there is a good choice.	It is too expensive.	There is not a lot of choice and the food is not healthy.
How many subjects do they study?	8	9	8
What is their favourite subject?	Art	Geography	Music
How many pupils are there in their classes?	25	47	18
What facilities are there?	Labs/computer rooms	Football pitch and basketball court	A big library with a lot of vocabulary.
What do they say about their teachers?	She likes them/they are understanding and patient.	They are approachable and they respect their pupils.	She doesn't like them. They are very strict/ give too much homework.
Do they wear a uniform?	No	No	Yes
What is their opinion of wearing a uniform?	It is a bad idea. She would prefer to wear a uniform because it is expensive to buy different clothes to be fashionable at school every day.	He feels comfortable not wearing one.	She doesn't like it/ it is awful. Everyone looks the same. She would prefer to wear comfortable/ fashionable clothes.
What do they like about school?	She can spend time with her friends. They chat and have a laugh at lunchtime.	That there is no uniform at school.	There are lots of sports clubs and a choir after lessons.
What do they not like about school?	There are not enough benches in the playground.	The rules are strict. You aren't allowed to use mobile phones or talk during lessons. There are not enough computers	Her parents pay for her books and jotters.

 **ACTIVITY:** The school system in Scotland – Le système scolaire en Écosse

1. Oban/West of Scotland
2. Quite big
3. 800 pupils
4. Modern
5. 8.50am/3.30pm (08:50/15:30)
6. 1.10pm (13:10)
7. Normally they eat at the canteen (there is a good choice and it is not expensive). Sometimes pupils go to the shops to buy a sandwich and a drink.
8. 6
9. 30
10. It is chic/smart/elegant.
11. The pupils get on well with the teachers/there are a lot of extra-curricular activities.
12. The rules are strict/you don't have a lot of freedom.

Improving education systems – Améliorer les systèmes scolaires (pp58–59)

 **ACTIVITY:** My preferences at school – Mes préferénces au lycée

Complaints	Ideal situations
Lessons are boring.	I would like interesting and fun lessons.
I find the traditional subjects quite boring.	I would like to study more dynamic and modern subjects like dance.
There are 30 pupils in my class.	I prefer to be in a class with 20 pupils.
Lessons start at nine o'clock.	I would like to start at eleven o'clock.
Lessons finish at half past three.	I would like to finish at one o'clock.
We have 45 minutes for lunch.	I would like to have two hours for lunch.
We have a 15 minute break.	I would prefer a break of half an hour.
It is too expensive and there is not enough choice in the canteen.	I would like to have cheaper food and more choice in the canteen.
There are not enough computers.	I would like to have more IT rooms.
There are not enough sports facilities.	I would like to have more sports facilities.
The library is small and there is not enough of a choice of books	I would like a big library with a good choice of books.
The rules are too strict	I would like less rules at school
Pupils don't have a lot of freedom.	I would like to have more freedom at school.
We must wear uniform, which is awful.	I would like to wear what I want to school.
We don't have to wear a uniform.	I would like to wear a uniform because then everyone is equal.
My teachers are very strict.	I prefer teachers who are relaxed.
Teachers give us too much homework.	I would like teachers who would never give homework.

 ACTIVITY The rules –
Le règlement

Antoine: mauvais; règles; écouter; boire; portable; juste.

Bernadette mauvaise; ressemble; d'individualité; coûte; sociales; perd.

Stéphanie élèves; serviables; devoirs; utiles; portable; saine.

EMPLOYABILITY

Different jobs – Les emplois différents (pp60–61)

 ACTIVITY Where do you work? –
Où travailles-tu?

1. A 2. G 3. F 4. D 5. H 6. C 7. E 8. B

 ACTIVITY Qualities for different jobs – Les qualités pour les emplois différents

Pharmacien(ne)	2; 3; 6; 7; 8; 9; 11
Journaliste	2; 3; 7; 8; 9; 10; 11; 12
Pompier	1; 2; 4; 7; 9; 11
Réceptionniste	2; 3; 7; 8; 9; 10; 11; 12

 ACTIVITY Revision – La révision

2. (a) I would like to be a doctor. It is necessary to pass my exams and I have to get good grades. To be a doctor, you have to have patience, you have to communicate well with sick people and have the ability to work under pressure.

   (b) I would like to be a musician. You have to be creative and have a lot of talent, enthusiasm and energy. I would like to know how to speak a foreign language because it is useful if you have the opportunity to travel around the world.

   (c) In the future I would like to be a vet. You have to be hard-working, polite and organised. You must know how to communicate with others and you must love animals. Furthermore, it is important to have a good memory.

   (d) In the future, I would like to be an air hostess. It is necessary to be fit, sociable and polite. I would like to travel around the world and perhaps I will live abroad. You must work in a team and like working with the public.

Part-time jobs – Les petits boulots 1 (pp62–63)

 ACTIVITY My part-time job –
Mon petit boulot

1. Café/waiter
2. Hotel/receptionist
3. Shop/sales assistant
4. Supermarket/cashier
5. Look after neighbours children/babysitter

 ACTIVITY What do you do at work? – Qu'est-ce que tu fais au travail?

1. Vendeur/vendeuse
2. Vendeur/vendeuse/réceptionniste/caissier/caissière/serveur/serveuse
3. Vendeur/vendeuse/réceptionniste/caissier/caissière/serveur/serveuse
4. Caissier/caissière/serveur/serveuse/vendeur/vendeuse

5. Baby-sitter
6. Caissier/caissière/vendeur/vendeuse/serveur/serveuse
7. Réceptionniste
8. Réceptionniste
9. Serveur/serveuse
10. Réceptionniste/serveur/serveuse
11. Réceptionniste
12. Baby-sitter

 ACTIVITY When do you work? –
Quand est-ce que tu travailles?

A. 1. Monday afternoon; Wednesday evening; 2. 8 hours per week; 3. €5.80 per hour 4. By bus and train

B. 1. Saturday from 9am to 5pm; Sunday from midday to 4pm; 2. 12 hours per week; 3. €6.35 per hour 4. By car.

C. 1. Thursday after lessons, Friday evening 2. 6 hours per week 3. €7.15 per hour 4. By bike.

D. 1. Twice a week Sunday morning; Tuesday afternoon 2. 5 hours per week 3. €6.95 per hour 4. On foot.

Part-time jobs – Les petits boulots 2 (pp64–65)

ACTIVITY Opinions – Les opinions

1. I (positive)
2. N (positive)
3. M (positive)
4. F (negative)
5. L (negative)
6. R (negative)
7. D (negative)
8. U (positive)
9. T (positive)
10. G (positive)
11. B (positive)
12. Q (positive)
13. A (positive)
14. J (negative)
15. C (negative)
16. O (negative)
17. E (positive)
18. S (negative)
19. H (negative)
20. K (negative)
21. P (negative)

ACTIVITY Revision – La révision

1. I am a waitress in a café in the town centre. I have to prepare tea and coffee and serve customers. I work three times per week and I earn €5.70 per hour. I like my job because it is easy and fun. I am always very busy therefore the time passes quickly. Furthermore my boss is patient and my colleagues are helpful. I never get bored, which is great!

2. I work as a sales person in a clothes chop. I have to help customers, tidy the shop and handle money. What I like the most is that I get reductions and the customers are polite. However, I hate my job because my boss is too strict and impatient. Furthermore I have to work four times a week therefore I don't have enough free time. Finally, my part time job is badly paid; I only earn €5.20 per hour.

3. I am a receptionist in a hotel at the seaside. I have to answer the phone, solve problems and take reservations. I work every Saturday and I do nine hours per week. It is well paid because I earn €7.40 per hour. It's great because I also get tips. My boss is very nice and my colleagues are kind.

ACTIVITY Studying and working – Étudier et travailler

Sophie

Advantages:

- She has increased her confidence
- She is more mature
- She has her own money

Disadvantage:

- She is too tired to go out (in the week)

Christian

Disadvantages:

- He thinks young people should enjoy their youth

APPENDICES

- As there are too many unemployed people, it is unfair to give a job to a student

Céline

Advantages:

- She can buy clothes to go out with her friends
- Her job gives her independence
- She can spend money how she wants
- She doesn't completely depend on her parents

Disadvantages:

- She has to work 20 hours per week which is too much
- Difficult to find the balance between her studies and work
- Often she doesn't have enough time to complete homework because she has to work
- As a consequence her teachers are not happy.

Pierre

Advantages:

- It is well paid
- He doesn't need to work too many hours.
- He also gets tips and that helps his financial situation.
- Colleagues are fun and he has made friends which is great as he lives far away from his school friends.
- He can eat what he wants at work and therefore he can save money

Disadvantages:

- The hours are long and he has to work until midnight
- He is often tired
- He finds it difficult to concentrate during lessons.
- His friends go out and he has to work

Work experience – Mon stage en entreprise (pp66–67)

 **ACTIVITY** My work experience – Mon stage en entreprise

	Where did they work?	When did they start?	When did they finish?	What did they do?	What did they like?	What did they not like?	Overall opinion
Marion	Sports shop	8.30am	1600 4pm	Served customers Worked at the till	Contact with the public	Boss was unpleasant	Good Varied
Stéphane	Fast -food restaurant	10am	1900 7pm	Prepared chips and hamburgers	Working in a team	The day was long He was very tired	Bad/ Boring/ monotonous
Laure	Hair dressing salon	9am	1800 6pm	Answered the phone Welcomed customers	Customers were kind Boss was patient and understanding	It was a long day Not a lot of breaks for staff	Good experience Easy
Marcus	Office/ A large company	9am	1730 5.30pm	Filed documents Sent emails	Got on well with his colleagues Learned a lot	Working alone	Good/ interesting

Work experience activities – Les activités pendant un stage (pp70–71)

 **ACTIVITY** Positive or negative – Positif ou négatif

Positif: 1.; 4.; 5.; 6.; 8.; 9.; 10.   Négatif: 2.; 3.; 7.; 11.; 12.

 **ACTIVITY** Who is it? – C'est qui?

1. Luc
2. Stéphanie
3. Luc
4. Marc
5. Marc
6. Stéphanie
7. Marc
8. Luc
9. Stéphanie
10. Stéphanie

 **ACTIVITY** Revision – La révision

1. At a primary school
2. By bus and on foot
3. 30 minutes
4. 8.45am
5. 3.10pm
6. Break at 10.30am. Lunch break at 1.00pm.
7. Helping children to read in small groups; organising games; helping pupils with their work; helped pupils to tidy the classroom; file teachers' documents.
8. To communicate well with children/to organise activities.
9. Yes, the children were really fun/funny and full of life; it was useful and varied.
10. To become a primary teacher.

My future plans – Mes projets pour l'avenir (pp72–73)

 **ACTIVITY** My ideal job – Mon métier idéal

A. 1. He wants to be a tour guide.

2. Tourism interests him a lot; good at foreign languages and it is useful to be able to communicate with people from different countries; he has the personal qualities for this job; he is polite, sociable and likes to work in a team; he can meet a lot of new people; he will perhaps have the opportunity to travel abroad with groups of tourists.

3. He will go to college to study tourism.

B. 1. He wants to study medicine to become a doctor.

2. He always gets good marks in sciences; people say he is nice, helpful and understanding; he can care for sick people; it is a varied and interesting job; he will earn a lot of money.

3. He will continue his studies at university and get a degree in medicine.

C. 1. She wants to be a PE teacher.

2. She wants to work in the fresh air with young people; she does not want to spend time behind a computer; she wants to be outside; tennis is her passion; PE is her favourite subject at school; she is capable of this job because she is patient, energetic and dynamic; she will get a good salary and she will have long holidays.

3. She will go to university to study education/teaching.

 **My future plans – Mes projets pour l'avenir**

1. Je travaillerai avec le public, peut-être dans un magasin, parce que j'aime le contact avec d'autres personnes.

   I will work with the public, perhaps in a shop because I like the contact with other people.

2. Je serai cuisinier dans un grand restaurant célèbre.

   I will be a chef in a big, famous restaurant.

3. J'ai envie de soigner les malades car ça me donnera l'occasion d'aider différentes personnes.

   I want to care for sick people because that will give me an opportunity to help different people.

4. Je travaillerai pour une grande entreprise internationale, peut-être dans le secteur informatique.

   I will work in a large international company, perhaps in the computing sector.

5. Je ferai un métier créatif parce que j'adore le dessin.

   I will do a creative job because I love art.

6. Je ne sais pas encore ce que je ferai à l'avenir mais je sais que j'habiterai à l'étranger.

   I don't know yet what I will do in the future but I know that I will live abroad.

7. Je chercherai un métier qui me permettra de voyager autour du monde.

   I will look for a job which will allow me to travel around the world.

8. Je ferai un diplôme au lycée technique.

   I will do a diploma at FE college.

9. Si je réussis à mes examens, j'irai à la faculté et je continuerai mes études.

   If I pass my exams, I will go to university and I will continue my studies.

10. Je serai joueur de basket professionnel et je gagnerai beaucoup d'argent.

    I will be a professional basketball player and I will earn a lot of money.

 **What would you do? – Qu'est-ce que tu ferais?**

1. Je travaillerais avec le public, peut-être dans un magasin, parce que j'aime le contact avec d'autres personnes.

   I would work with the public, perhaps in a shop because I like the contact with other people.

2. Je serais cuisinier dans un grand restaurant célèbre.

   I would be a chef in a big, famous restaurant.

3. J'ai envie de soigner les malades car ça me donnerait l'occasion d'aider différentes personnes.

   I want to care for sick people because that would give me an opportunity to help different people.

4. Je travaillerais pour une grande entreprise internationale, peut-être dans le secteur informatique.

   I would work in a large international company, perhaps in the computing sector.

5. Je ferais un métier créatif parce que j'adore le dessin.

   I would do a creative job because I love art.

6. Je ne sais pas encore ce que je ferais à l'avenir mais je sais que j'habiterai à l'étranger.

   I don't know yet what I would do in the future but I know that I will live abroad.

7. Je chercherais un métier qui me permettrait de voyager autour du monde.

   I would look for a job which would allow me to travel around the world.

8. Je ferais un diplôme au lycée technique.

   I would do a diploma at FE college.

9. Si je réussis à mes examens, j'irais à la faculté et je continuerais mes études.

   If I pass my exams, I would go to university and I would continue my studies.

10. Je serais joueur de basket professionnel et je gagnerais beaucoup d'argent.

    I would be a professional basketball player and I would earn a lot of money.

CULTURE

Holidays – Les vacances 1 (pp74–75)

 **With whom – Avec qui**

There are three words for my in French. These are <u>mon</u>, <u>ma</u> and <u>mes</u>. We use "ma" for <u>feminine</u> words, <u>mon</u> for masculine words and <u>mes</u> for plural words.

 **For how long? – Pendant combien de temps?**

1. Last summer I went to Lyon in France for two weeks with my friends.

2. During the summer holidays I went with my family to the seaside in Spain.

3. At Christmas time I spent two weeks in a small village in Canada with my mum.

4. Three years ago I went alone to the mountains in Switzerland for a month.

 **Accommodation – Logement**

Dans un hôtel	(all the options are possible – except "une grande cuisine")
Dans une auberge de jeunesse	(all the options are possible – except "une grande cuisine"/"une salle de gym"/"des courts de tennis")
Dans un camping	(all the options are possible – except "une grande cuisine", "un balcon", "ma propre chambre")
Dans un gîte	(all options are possible, except « un restaurant », « un bar » « une piste de danse »)
Chez la famille	(all the options are possible – except "un restaurant, un bar, une salle de gym, une piste de danse")
Chez des amis	(all the options are possible – except "un restaurant, un bar, une salle de gym, une piste de danse")

Holidays – Les vacances 2 (pp76–77)

 **Grammar/translation activity – Une exercice de grammaire/traduction**

1. suis allée; passait; faire du ski; allait; manger; est allé;acheter.

2. suis parti; allait; restait; bronzer; passait; adore danser; a fait de la planche à voile.

3. suis allé; se promenait; visitait; buvait; est allé; visiter; faire du shopping.

 **Opinions of the trip– Opinion sur le voyage**

Positive	Negative
C'était super	Je n'y retournerai pas
Le personnel était très serviable	Les gens étaient très impolis
Je me suis bien amusé(e)	C'était ennuyeux
C'était intéressant	La nourriture n'était pas très bonne
C'était amusant	C'était nul!
Je recommanderais ce genre de voyage	Il pleuvait tous les jours
Les gens étaient très accueillants	Les gens n'étaient pas gentils
La nourriture était délicieuse	Il n'y avait rien à faire
Les gens étaient très aimables	C'était sale

APPENDICES

 ACTIVITY: The importance of travel – L'importance de voyager

J'adore voyager parce qu'/car on se fait de nouveaux amis.

J'aime aller à l'étranger parce qu'/car on découvre de nouvelles cultures et traditions.

J'aime partir en vacances parce qu'/car on se détend et qu' on oublie la vie quotidienne.

J'aime visiter des pays étrangers parce qu'/car on profite du beau temps.

Il est important de voyager pour voir comment vivent d'autres personnes.

À mon avis voyager est un bon moyen de découvrir d'autres pays et de parler une autre langue.

 ACTIVITY: Cédric's best holiday – Les meilleures vacances de Cédric

Quand – when	• Last April
Où – where	• Morocco – seaside
Avec qui – with whom	• Friends
Pendant combien de temps – for how long	• A week
Logement – accommodation	• Luxury hotel – lovely • Two big swimming pools, a gym, three restaurants, two bars • Bedrooms – very big with a balcony and view of the sea
Activités – activities	• Swimming in swimming pool, sunbathing • Afternoons walking next to the water or drinking mint tea in the cafés • One day went to the Souk (big market); bought Moroccan cakes and presents for family and friends • One evening went to a typical restaurant and saw belly dancers
Opinion – opinion	• Had a great time • People really welcoming and spoke French • Very important to travel as we discover a new culture, see how other people live and holidays allow us to relax

Events, literature and film – Les traditions, la littérature et les films 1 (pp78–79)

 ACTIVITY: Traditions and special events – Les traditions et événements spéciaux

Verb	English
fêter	to celebrate
manger	to eat
boire	to drink
danser	to dance
chanter	to sing
se déguiser	to dress up
prier	to pray

Noun	English
une fête	a party/celebration
des cadeaux	presents

un gâteau	a cake
les feux d'artifice	fireworks
du champagne	champagne
un déguisement	a fancy dress

 ACTIVITY: What is the book/film about? – De quoi parle le film/le livre?

The book/film is set in the 20th century and takes place in the south of France.

The book/film talks about...

The book/film tells the story of...

 ACTIVITY: Your favourite characters – Tes personnages préférés

Masculine	Féminine	English
beau	belle	good-looking/beautiful
marrant	marrante	funny
méchant	méchante	nasty
crédible	crédible	believable
ennuyeux	ennuyeuse	boring
jeune	jeune	young
vieux	vieille	old

 ACTIVITY: Your opinions – Ton opinion

Positive

What I really liked is/was ...

I really liked the book/film because...

I had never read/seen this type of book/film but I would recommend it because the story is really interesting.

I learned a lot/I discovered a lot about French culture for example, French people attach a lot of importance to spending time with family around a big meal.

Normally I never watch science/love/action films but I really liked this film.

I really liked this film and I will watch other films of this type in the future.

I would recommend this book/film because the story interested me a lot and I liked the actors a lot.

Negative

I found this film a bit long but I really liked the actors and the story.

I didn't like this book/film because the story was very boring.

I was disappointed by this book/film.

I wouldn't recommend this book/film because it wasn't interesting and nothing happened.

I didn't like this film because I don't like action films which are too violent.

Events, literature and film – Les traditions, la littérature et les films 2 (pp80–81)

 ACTIVITY: Opinions on a film – Avis sur un film

1. Last week
2. A small village in the south of England

3. Four friends who haven't seen each other for 15 years/who meet up for a weekend

4. (a) They get on well/reminisce about their youth.

   (b) Tensions begin between them.

   (c) They realise their lives have changed. They have nothing in common.

5. Good actress, believable.

6. He likes watching films with subtitles as they help improve his English.

 **ACTIVITY** Sylvie's opinion on a book – L'avis de Sylvie sur un livre

1.	intéressant	5.	parlent	9.	marrant
2.	2005	6.	mois	10.	beaucoup
3.	retraités	7.	commencent	11.	française
4.	début	8.	préféré	12.	drôle

COURSE ASSESSMENT: WRITING

Bullet point 2: School/college/education experience until now 2 (pp88–89)

THINGS TO DO AND THINK ABOUT

1. grande; cent; amis; entends; dernière; allemand; étudie; anglais; étrangères; savoir; jours; trouve; sévère; devoirs; quitterai; français; travailler; étranger.

2. élève; train; grand; vieux; toujours; dernier; musique; année; histoire; matière; forte; notes; contre; difficile; avis; avenir; droit; propre; argent.

Bullet point 3: Skills/interests you have which make you right for the job (pp90–91)

THINGS TO DO AND THINK ABOUT

1. Je voudrais postuler pour cet emploi car j'aimerais améliorer mon français.

2. J'adore voyager et ce poste me donnerait l'occasion de découvrir une nouvelle culture.

3. Je serais très travailleur (se) et j'adore travailler en équipe.

4. Je suis la personne idéale pour ce poste car je suis poli(e) et je m'entends bien avec tout le monde.

5. Quand je quitterai l'école, j'aimerais voyager et travailler à l'étranger.

6. Pendant mon temps libre j'adore faire du sport. Je fais partie d'un club de hockey et je m'entraîne chaque weekend.

7. Quand j'ai du temps libre j'aime faire de longues promenades avec mes chiens. Ça me maintient en forme et j'aime être en plein air.

8. Je m'intéresse beaucoup à la musique et en ce moment j'apprends à jouer de la flûte.

9. Je me passionne pour l'art et j'adore passer mon temps à visiter les galeries d'art.

10. Quand il fait beau j'adore faire de l'équitation / des randonnées à cheval à la campagne.

Bullet point 4: Related work experience (pp92–93)

 **ACTIVITY** What you did – Ce que vous avez fait

mettre les tables	set the tables
débarrasser les tables	clear the tables
classer les dossiers	sort out the files
servir les clients	serve customers
m'occuper des enfants	look after the children

répondre au téléphone	answer the phone
jouer avec les enfants	play with children
prendre des commandes	take orders
accueillir les clients	welcome customers

 **ACTIVITY** Yannick's work experience

1. *Any one from:* Last year/during Easter holidays.

2. *Any two from:* A hotel/centre of Toulouse/in a restaurant.

3. Set the tables, welcome the customers, take orders.

4. *Any three from:* All customers were nice/left him good tips/he got on with everyone/learnt a lot about restaurant work.

COURSE ASSESSMENT: LISTENING

Listening activities 1 (pp98–99)

 **ACTIVITY** 1. Family and friends – La famille et les amis

Section 1

1. *Any one from:* She is very understanding/always available to help her

2. *Any one from:* She helps her with her homework/when she has problems with her friends

3. *Any two from:* He is annoying/he teases her (in front of her friends)/he uses her computer (without asking for permission)

4. (a) *Any one from:* Her father is too protective/he doesn't let her go out with her friends (during the week)

   (b) *Any two from:* She respects her private life/she gives her a lot of freedom/they spend a lot of time together

5. *Statement 2:* She has positive and negative relationships with her family

Section 2

1. (a) *Any one from:* During the holidays/Friday evenings

   (b) *Any one from:* (Inviting her friends over to) watch a film/eat pizza

2. *Any two from:* Someone who understands her/someone who shares her interests/someone she can confide in

3. *Any two from:* Someone who criticises her/someone who is in a bad mood (all the time)/someone who is selfish

4. Smoke/drink alcohol

5. *Any two from:* She can wear what she wants/like different films/have (her own) opinions

6. *Any two from:* She can talk to her (about everything)/she is patient/she gives her good advice

 **ACTIVITY** 2. Leisure and Health – Les loisirs et la santé

Section 1

1. *Any two from:* They are delicious/they are healthy/they always contain vegetables

2. *Any two from:* Crisps/sweets/cakes

3. *Any two from:* Smoking is expensive/the smell is unpleasant/it's dangerous for your lungs

4. *Any one from:* (It helps them) to relax/to become (more) sociable

5. *Statement 2:* Leading a healthy lifestyle is important

APPENDICES

Section 2

1. Three times per week

2. *Any two from:* It's tiring/she has to run a lot/after training she (always) wants to sleep

3. *Any one from:* She can make new friends/it's fun

4. (a) *Any one from:* Her mother is generous/her mother (always) buys her clothes

   (b) *Any one from:* They both like horror films/he treats her to a hamburger

5. (a) *Any one from:* He has to travel abroad often/with his work

   (b) *Any one from:* Water sports/windsurfing

6. The seaside/the west of Morocco

7. *Any two from:* The people are welcoming/they speak French/the weather is good

 3. Technology and TV/film – La technologie, la télé et les films

Section 1

1. *Any two from:* You can stay in contact with family/friends (from anywhere)/buy things online/download films/music (cheaply)

2. *Any two from:* You have to be careful when you chat online/personal information can be stolen/you can get a headache (if you stay on for a long time)

3. *Any two from:* Many young people can't live without their mobile phone/spend less time reading/spend less time speaking face to face (with friends)

4. Everyone needs to be aware of the dangers

5. *Statement 1:* Overall he thinks technology is a good thing

Section 2

1. It's her birthday

2. *Any one from:* The suspense/trying to guess the killer

3. *Statements 1 and 4:* She loves the atmosphere (and) she loves watching films on a big screen

4. *Any two from:* She has exams/she spends a lot of time revising/doing homework

5. (a) *Any one from:* It helps her to relax/there's no need to concentrate

   (b) *Any one from:* She learns things/she tries to answer the questions

6. *Any two from:* You can see the candidates' progress/they make good things to eat/you can try the recipes

7. (a) *Any one from:* She's not sporty/they are boring

   (b) *Any one from:* They are every ten minutes/rubbish

Listening activities 2 (pp100–101)

 4. Home area and the environment Où j'habite et l'environnement

Section 1

1. Eight years

2. *Any one from:* Walking his dog/eating in one of the restaurants

3. *Any two from:* Too many tourists in summer/litter on the ground/too much pollution (because of cars)

4. *Any two from:* There was nothing to do (for young people)/the cinema was an hour away/there was no public transport

---

5. *Any one from:* He loves the British sense of humour/he can improve his English

6. *Statement 2:* He loves living in a big town

Section 2

1. *Any one from:* In a little village/in the mountains

2. *Statements 1 and 3:* They live on a farm (and) they have a swimming pool

3. *Any two from:* They are young at heart/she can talk to them about anything/her cousin lives in the house opposite

4. (a) *Any one from:* She went shopping (or to the market)/she helped her grandfather with the animals

   (b) She had a barbecue (at her cousin's house)

5. She can ski in winter/go hillwalking in summer

6. *Any one from:* She has to get up early to go to school/school is an hour away

7. *Any two from:* The scenery is lovely/she can relax/she feels less stressed

 5. Experience at school and future plans – La vie scolaire et les projets pour l'avenir

Section 1

1. *Any two from:* It has a good atmosphere/it's lively/there's a good relationship with the teachers

2. School starts (lessons start) at 8am/school finishes at 4pm/she spends eight hours at school/she gets (at least) two hours' homework/she gets a lot of homework

3. *Any one from:* She gets good marks/she is creative

4. *Any two from:* He inspires them/he prepares his lessons (well)/he explains things clearly

5. *Statement 3:* She likes it but she gets too much homework

Section 2

1. (a) *Any one from:* To relax/go out with her friends

   (b) She is passionate about it/she spends all her pocket money on clothes (or shoes)

2. *Any one from:* She doesn't have enough money/she doesn't have a part-time job

3. (a) *Any two from:* She has a good relationship with them/they have a laugh/they have a lot in common

   (b) *Any one from:* Her mother makes (or prepares) meals/her mother does her laundry

4. (a) clothes shop

   (b) Save money/find a flat (or apartment)

5. *Any two from:* Go into town/go shopping/go to (or chat in) cafés

 6. Job searches and interviews – La recherche d'emploi et les entretiens

Section 1

1. To pay his mobile phone bill/save for studies (or university)

2. Office secretaries/waiters

3. *Any one from:* He doesn't have experience/he is not interested in these types of job

4. He will be able to work with children/he likes working outside

5. *Statement 1:* It has been quite difficult to find a job

Section 2

1. *Any two from:* Do online research/find information about the company/ prepare questions

2. *Statement 3:* A black jumper

3. *Any two from:* It's in an office/in the town centre/15 minutes from her house by bus

4. €9.00 <u>per hour</u>

5. *Any two from:* Four days a week/eight hours a day/45 minutes for lunch

6. *Any two from:* Someone who can work in a team/someone you can trust/ someone who is punctual

7. *Any two from:* She can earn her own money/she will be more independent/ she can make new friends

 **ACTIVITY** 7. Holidays – Les vacances

Section 1

1. *Any two from:* It has three floors/four bedrooms/two bathrooms

2. *Any two from:* She is the same age/she is funny/they can talk about everything together

3. (a) *Any one from:* Swim in the pool/go for bike rides (in the countryside)

   (b) *Any one from:* Stay at home/play cards

4. She has to leave her dog/she misses her dog

5. *Statement 3:* She loves going on holiday to her aunt's

Section 2

1. Two weeks (or 15 days)

2. *Any two from:* They could get up late/eat what they wanted/go to a club (without asking for permission)

3. *Any one from:* The plane was (two hours) late/they lost their bags (or luggage)

4. *Statements 2 and 4:* It was at the seaside (and) the room was clean

5. (a) *Any two from:* Not a lot/they swam in the sea/they played volleyball on the beach

   (b) *Any two from:* They went on excursions/visited <u>old</u> churches/visited <u>typical</u> villages

6. *Any two from:* The people are welcoming/you can improve your Spanish/ you can meet new people

GLOSSARY

adjectives – describe a noun e.g. big – grand; small – petit

adverbs – describe/modify verbs, adjectives and other adverbs e.g. slowly – lentement; quickly – rapidement

avoir phrases – phrases in French which use the verb avoir, e.g. avoir faim – to be hungry

comparatives – the comparison of two or more nouns in terms of more or less, greater or lesser, we normally add 'er' to the end of an adjective or adverb to make the comparison, e.g. John is taller than Brian – John est plus grand que Brian

conditional tense – used to describe what someone would do or what would happen e.g. I would play football – je jouerais au foot

conjunctions – linking words or connectors e.g. and – et; but – mais; however – pourtant

Definite article – 'the' in English; le, la, l', les in French

false friends – a word that looks similar in two languages but means different things in each language e.g. sensible means sensitive in French

imperfect tense – used to describe a past, repeated action, what used to happen, what was happening or what something was like in the past e.g. I used to play/was playing football – je jouais au foot

indefinite article – 'a' or 'an' in English, 'un' or 'une' in French e.g. he has a car – il a une voiture

infinitive – the name/title/basic form of a verb that doesn't specify who is doing the verb (the subject) or when the verb is carried out (tense). In English, the infinitive has the word 'to' in front of it, e.g. to play; in French the infinitive of regular verbs will end in -er, -ir, -re e.g jouer, finir, vendre

intensifiers – a word that adds force to a verb, adjective or adverb e.g. really – vraiment, too – trop

irregular past participles – verbs in their past form that do not follow the usual pattern e.g. in English when the past part of the verb doesn't end in -ed e.g. seen- vu; done- fait

irregular verbs – verbs that don't follow a regular pattern when they are conjugated (put in different forms in different tenses) e.g. to have – avoir; to be – être

KAL – knowledge about language e.g. vocabulary, grammar, tenses

modal verbs – a verb that combines with another verb to indicate mood, necessity or possibility e.g. to want to – vouloir; to have to – devoir; to be able to – pouvoir

near future tense – used to describe what someone will do or what will happen in the future, e.g. I will play football – je jouerai au foot

negatives – words which negate the verb e.g. I don't play – je ne joue pas; he doesn't like – il n'aime pas; I never go – je ne vais jamais

nouns – name a person, place, thing, quality or action e.g. people – les gens; classroom – la salle de classe; pencil – le crayon

past participle – verbs in their past form. In English we usually add -ed to the end of the verb and in French, we chop off the ending of the verb and for -er verbs, we add é e.g. joué- played; for -ir verbs we add i e.g. fini – finished; and for -re verbs we add -u e.g. répondu – answered

perfect tense – used to describe a past completed action e.g. I (have) played – j'ai joué

prepositions – a word that indicates the relationship between a noun or pronoun and other words in a sentence e.g. the book is on the table – le livre est sur la table

present tense – used to describe what usually happens or what is happening in the present e.g. I eat/ I am eating – je mange

Pronoun – a word that takes the place of a noun e.g. John eats chocolate can be changed to 'he eats it'

reflexive verbs – verbs that are done to oneself e.g. to wash oneself – se laver; I wash myself – je me lave

regular verbs – verbs that follow a pattern when conjugated (put in different forms in different tenses) e.g. to play – jouer

relative pronouns – used to link what is stated in different clauses e.g. who, that, which, whom, whose, where, when. I have a dog who is called Max – j'ai un chien qui s'appelle Max

simple future tense – used to describe what is going to happen or what someone is going to do in the future e.g. I am going to play football – je vais jouer au foot

subject pronouns – the person or thing that does the verb e.g. I – je; you – tu; he – il; she – elle etc.

superlatives – used in comparisons to show which noun is the most or least of a quality or characteristic e.g. the tallest – le plus grand

tense – indicates when the verb takes place (present/past/future)

Verbs – action words e.g. I play football – je joue au foot (play is the verb)